# CYBER ATTACK PREVENTION

## Why Your IT Department Must Partner with a Third-Party Cyber Security Firm



CHRIS WISER

Published by Prominence Publishing,
www.prominencepublishing.com

Cyber Attack Prevention -- 1st ed.

ISBN: 978-1-990830-25-9

# Contents


Foreword — By Chris Wiser ........ 1

Why CEOs Need to Understand Cyber Security Risks — By Darin Schoumaker ........ 5

It's Not IF, but WHEN You're Breached — By Jake McCann ........ 19

5 Ways Your Business Can Reduce Cyber Risk — By Nick D'Emanuele ........ 39

The Cyber Security Guide: 5 Things Your Business NEEDS Now — By Mike Bloomfield ........ 57

IT Negligence: The Secret Business Killer — By Brett Gallant ........ 77

The Importance of Securing Your Private Business Data — By Linwood Wright ........ 93

The Anatomy of a Cyber-Attack: A Guide for Executives — By Chris Burns ........ 115

Is Your Business Cyber-Attack Ready? — By Bill Bunnell ........ 129

Real-Life Cyber Attacks — By Dan DeFay ........ 149

Cyber Security for Healthcare Providers — By Ken Satkunam ........ 159

How Vulnerable is Your Business to Hackers? — By James Forbis ........ 177

# Foreword

**By Chris Wiser**

Most of the time, Information Technology is thought of more as an expense than a necessity, which is why most business owners continue to look the other way when it comes to implementing a strong cyber security plan for their business. Today, cybercrime affects all businesses, regardless of size or location, and as technology advances and we continue to live in a remote, digital world, it is crucial to understand the NEED for Cyber Security. The fact of the matter is that business owners who are not protecting their business data, their assets and their employees are at **great risk.**

Currently, what steps are you taking to ensure your business is safe from hackers and the evolving threat of cyber security?

As a business owner, if you cannot clearly define the general cyber security approach your business is using to secure assets and confidential data on your business network, this is a major concern.

As cybercrime becomes a commonality, the likelihood that your business will be attacked is high – in our industry we like to use the phrase:

"It's not **IF** but **WHEN** your business will be attacked."

Today, businesses need to assume that they will be breached by hackers at some point in their future. As cybercriminals continue to evolve their tactics, business owners will need to increase security measures to not only safeguard their financial assets, but also their business data from being stolen or compromised.

Too many times we hear of business owners turning their cheek to implementing cyber security measures to then have their business completely devastated by a cyber-attack.

How much can your business afford to lose in terms of both time and money to stay in business?

Protecting your business from cyberthreats is crucial to your ongoing success and should be your top priority as a business owner. Most business owners are familiar with the term cyber security, but do not completely understand the need for it in their business.

If you have been turning your head the other way when it comes to cyber security, it is crucial to understand that NO BUSINESS is too small or too large to avoid this, and you need to start preparing for the worst-case scenario.

At the very least, your business should hire a third-party cyber security expert, implement a strong cyber security plan and take necessary steps to protect your business from cybercrime.

If you are a business owner, the time is NOW to start caring about your business and take Cyber security seriously!

Chris Wiser, CEO,
7 Figure MSP

Speaker/Trainer/

Entrepreneur/ Coach

# Why CEOs Need to Understand Cyber Security Risks

**By Darin Schoumaker**

As the world becomes increasingly digital, cyber security threats are becoming more sophisticated and frequent. Cyber-attacks can cause significant financial and reputational damage to organizations, making cyber security a top priority for companies of all sizes. In the past, cyber security was seen as the responsibility of the IT department, but today, it's essential that CEOs and other senior executives also have a deep understanding of cyber security risks and their potential impact on their business.

Cyber security risks can come in many forms including phishing attacks, ransomware, data breaches, and more. These threats can compromise sensitive company and customer data, disrupt business operations, and even result in legal or regulatory penalties. In some cases, a single cyber-attack can be enough to cause irreparable damage to a company's reputation and financial standing.

CEOs play a critical role in managing cyber security risks by setting the tone at the top and ensuring that their organization has a comprehensive cyber security strategy in place. They need to understand the risks facing their organization and be able to make informed decisions about how to mitigate them. This includes allocating resources to cyber security initiatives, establishing policies and procedures to protect against threats, and implementing training programs to educate employees on how to identify and respond to cyber security risks.

CEOs who fail to prioritize cyber security risk management put their organizations at serious risk. They not only expose sensitive data to potential breaches but also risk regulatory fines, lawsuits, and damage to their reputation. In contrast, CEOs who prioritize cyber security can gain a competitive advantage by demonstrating to their customers and partners that they take data security seriously.

In this chapter, we will explore the various cyber security risks facing organizations today and discuss why CEOs need to have a deep understanding of these risks. We will also examine the key steps that CEOs specifically can take to ensure that their organization is prepared to defend against cyber-threats and protect sensitive data. By the end of this chapter, you'll have a better understanding of why cyber security is a critical issue for CEOs and what steps you can take to protect your organization from potential cyber-attacks.

## A Fictitious Fable

Once upon a time, there was a company with a CEO named John who had very little understanding of cyber security. He believed that the company's IT department was responsible for ensuring the security of their systems and that, as long as they had firewalls and antivirus software, they were safe from cyber threats.

One day, a cyber-criminal was able to gain access to the company's network and steal sensitive data including customer information and financial records. The breach was discovered when one of the company's clients reported suspicious activity on their account.

The IT department immediately reported the breach to the CEO, but he dismissed it as a minor incident and suggested that they simply change their passwords and continue with business as usual.

Unfortunately, the breach was much more severe than John had realized. The cyber-criminal had planted malware on the company's servers which allowed them to continue stealing data even after the initial breach had been discovered.

Over the next few weeks, the company's reputation was tarnished as more and more customers reported fraudulent activity on their accounts. Eventually, the company was forced to publicly acknowledge the breach and offer identity theft protection to all affected customers.

John was shocked by the extent of the damage and the negative impact it had on the company's bottom line. He realized too late that his lack of understanding of cyber security had left the company vulnerable to attack and that it was his responsibility as CEO to ensure the company's security measures were up to date and effective.

From that day forward, John made it a priority to educate himself and his staff on the importance of cyber security and to implement stronger security measures to prevent future breaches. He learned that cyber security is not just the responsibility of the IT department, but of the entire organization, and that it is essential for business leaders to stay informed and vigilant to protect their company's assets and reputation.

## Why Don't CEOs Care?

There are several reasons why CEOs may be unprepared for cyber security threats:

**Lack of Understanding:** Many CEOs do not have a strong understanding of the technical aspects of cyber security and the potential risks that their organizations face. This lack of knowledge can lead to a lack of prioritization of cyber security within their organizations.

**Overemphasis on Other Areas:** CEOs may be more focused on other areas of their businesses such as revenue growth, customer satisfaction, or cost-cutting and may not prioritize cyber security as a critical aspect of their business strategy.

**Resource Allocation:** Cyber security requires significant investments in terms of time, money, and resources. CEOs may be reluctant to allocate resources toward cyber security if they do not understand the potential risks and impacts of a cyber security breach.

**Complexity:** Cyber security is a complex and constantly evolving field, and CEOs may find it challenging to keep up with the latest threats and mitigation strategies.

**Perception of Invincibility:** Some CEOs may believe that their organization is immune to cyber-attacks or that the risks are overblown. This can lead to a false sense of security and a lack of preparedness.

To address these issues, it is essential that CEOs understand the importance of cyber security and prioritize it within their organizations. They should also seek out expert advice and resources to develop effective cyber security strategies and ensure that their organizations are adequately protected against potential threats.

As the world becomes increasingly digitized and interconnected, the risk of cyber-attacks has grown significantly. However, many CEOs still underestimate the potential impact of these attacks on their businesses. In fact, a recent study found that over 70% of CEOs believe their companies are adequately prepared to defend against cyber-attacks while only 30% of their IT professionals agreed.

This disconnect between CEOs and IT professionals can have serious consequences. Cyber-attacks can result in the loss of sensitive information, financial losses, reputational damage, and legal repercussions. Yet many CEOs fail to take adequate measures to protect their companies from these risks.

One reason for this lack of awareness may be the perception that cyber-attacks are the sole responsibility of IT departments. CEOs may believe that, as long as their companies have basic security measures in place, such as firewalls and antivirus software, they are protected. However, cyber-attacks are becoming increasingly sophisticated and complex, and even the most advanced security measures can be breached.

Another factor contributing to CEOs' lack of awareness is the speed at which technology is evolving. It can be difficult to keep up with the latest trends and threats, particularly for CEOs who are focused on running their businesses. Additionally, cyber security is often viewed as a cost center rather than a revenue generator, making it difficult to justify investments in preventative measures.

However, failing to invest in cyber security can be far more costly in the long run. A single cyber-attack can cost companies millions of dollars in lost revenue, legal fees, and damage to their reputations. Furthermore, the impact of cyber-attacks can extend beyond the company itself, affecting customers, suppliers, and other stakeholders.

To address this issue, it is important for CEOs to prioritize cyber security and ensure that it is integrated into their overall business strategy. This requires regular communication and collaboration between CEOs and IT professionals to identify and assess potential risks, develop comprehensive security plans, and regularly review and update those plans as new threats emerge.

Additionally, CEOs can seek out education and training opportunities to better understand the evolving cyber threat landscape and the steps they can take to protect their businesses. By prioritizing cyber security and taking proactive measures to defend against cyber-attacks, CEOs can better safeguard their companies and minimize the potential impact of these threats.

## Role of CEOs

CEOs play a critical role in managing cyber security risks by setting the tone at the top and ensuring that their organization has a comprehensive cyber security strategy in place. They need to understand the risks facing their organization and be able to make informed decisions about how to mitigate them. This includes allocating resources to cyber security initiatives, establishing policies and procedures to protect against threats, and implementing training programs to educate employees on how to identify and respond to cyber security risks.

## Consequences of Neglecting Cyber Security Risks

CEOs who fail to prioritize cyber security risk management put their organizations at serious risk. They not only expose sensitive data to potential breaches, but also risk regulatory fines, lawsuits, and damage to their reputation. In contrast, CEOs who prioritize cyber security can gain a competitive advantage by demonstrating to their customers and partners that they take data security seriously.

## Key Steps for CEOs to Ensure Cyber Security

To ensure that their organization is prepared to defend against cyber threats and protect sensitive data, CEOs can take several key steps. These steps include conducting regular risk assessments, establishing a comprehensive cyber security plan, implementing security controls, creating an incident response plan, and educating employees on cyber security best practices.

**Conducting Regular Risk Assessments:** Regular risk assessments are essential for identifying potential threats and vulnerabilities in an organization's IT infrastructure. By conducting these assessments, CEOs can gain a better understanding of the risks facing their organization and make informed decisions about how to mitigate them.

**Establishing a Comprehensive Cyber Security Plan**: A comprehensive cyber security plan should include policies and procedures for protecting sensitive data, guidelines for secure software development and system deployment, and an incident response plan.

**Implementing Security Controls:** To protect against cyber threats, CEOs should implement security controls such as firewalls, intrusion detection systems, and encryption technologies. These controls can help prevent unauthorized access to sensitive data and systems.

**Creating an Incident Response Plan:** An incident response plan outlines the steps that an organization should take in the event of a cyber security breach. It should include procedures for containing the breach, investigating the cause, and notifying stakeholders.

**Educating Employees on Cyber Security Best Practices:** Employees are often the weakest link in an organization's cyber security defenses. CEOs should ensure that all employees receive regular training on cyber security best practices such as how to identify phishing emails and how to create strong passwords.

## Conclusion

CEOs who prioritize cyber security risk management can gain a competitive advantage by demonstrating to their customers and partners that they take data security seriously. By implementing a comprehensive cyber security plan and educating employees on best practices, CEOs can protect their organizations from potential cyber-attacks and the resulting financial and reputational damage.

IronHand Cyber Security understands the risks CEOs are facing. By performing a Cyber Risk Security Assessment, CEOs can better understand what is at risk and their current security posture for protecting themselves now and into the future. The proactive CEO will take a Cyber Risk Security Assessment to arm themselves with information necessary to protect their company and mitigate risks. IronHand Cyber Security can be the guide to navigating this technological maze.

Reach out to us:

https://ironhandcybersecurity.com/cybersecurity-risk-assessment

# About the Author

Darin Schoumaker is a renowned cyber security expert and technologist with over two decades of experience in the field. Throughout his career, Darin has dedicated himself to the protection of sensitive data and the prevention of cyber-attacks.

Darin's expertise in cyber security began in the late 1990s, when he first began working with computer networks and systems. As the internet grew in popularity and importance, Darin recognized the need for greater security measures to be implemented, and he quickly became an expert in the field of cyber security.

Over the years, Darin has worked for a variety of organizations, both large and small, helping them to implement and maintain robust cyber security systems. He has served as a consultant for major corporations, government agencies, and non-profit organizations, providing them with the expertise they need to protect their data and systems from cyber-attacks.

Darin is also a well-respected thought leader in the field of cyber security, and he has published numerous articles and given many talks on the subject. He is particularly interested in emerging threats such as cyber espionage, ransomware, and social engineering, and he is constantly seeking new and innovative ways to protect against them.

In addition to his work in cyber security, Darin is also an accomplished technologist, with expertise in a variety of areas including software development, cloud computing, and network architecture. He is a true multi-disciplinary talent, with the ability to combine his expertise in technology with his deep knowledge of cyber security to provide comprehensive solutions for his clients.

Overall, Darin Schoumaker is an accomplished cyber security expert and technologist, with a proven track record of success in the field. His dedication to protecting sensitive data and preventing cyber-attacks has made him a respected figure in the industry, and his innovative approaches to cyber security continue to set the standard for the field.

Darin can be reached as follows:

www.linkedin.com/in/darinschoumaker

www.ironhandcybersecurity.com

# It's Not IF, but WHEN You're Breached

**By Jake McCann**

## Why Having a Specialized Cyber Security IT Team is a Necessity

As a small business owner these days, it takes a great deal of proactivity and expertise to keep your business and its data safe from compromise. Such a task cannot be left to a single individual anymore. It's crucial to understand the importance of having a specialized cyber security IT team. In today's world, cyber security threats are a reality, and it's not a matter of if you'll be breached, but when.

As technology continues to advance, the risk of cyber-attacks on businesses is increasing at an alarming rate, making it even harder for businesses to secure their data. Regardless of the type of business you own, whether a small retail store or a large corporation, you are at risk of being attacked. According to recent studies, small businesses are the most targeted by cyber-criminals. Hackers are well aware that small businesses often lack the resources to implement robust security measures, making them the low hanging fruit. This is particularly true in the case of micro-businesses, which often lack the financial resources to hire dedicated IT staff or even an outsourced IT security team.

In this chapter, we will discuss why having a competent cyber security team is a necessity for small businesses of all varieties. We'll also reference real-world scenarios and the different types of attack vectors such as ransomware, phishing, and fileless malware. Further, we'll highlight the inevitability of succumbing to a cyber-attack altogether. Lastly, we'll discuss the need for advanced AI-based XDR protection and Zero Trust frameworks to prevent these cyber-attacks. Without a compilation of the above, the chance of becoming the next victim is almost imminent and unavoidable.

## The Attack Vectors

Cyber security attacks can take many forms with new and evolving attack vectors appearing all the time. Let's dive into a handful of these types of attacks and learn more about what we need to protect against them.

## Phishing

First up on the list is a highly popular and highly deadly attack vector — any and all forms of phishing. Phishing attacks are where attackers impersonate a trusted entity to trick victims into providing sensitive information, are also becoming more common. Attackers are now using the email addresses of compromised contacts to launch attacks, making it more difficult to identify malicious communications. Phishing can oftentimes lead to other types of attacks because it gives the threat actor a foothold to perform social engineering and potentially exploit the unsuspecting victims' systems, many times without any awareness that anything malicious is going on.

## BEC

Next up, we are going to go over BEC attacks. Business Email Compromises are often originally executed as a type of phishing attack that involves an attacker posing as a trusted individual or business and tricking victims into transferring funds, providing sensitive information, or carrying out other actions that benefit the attacker like clicking on hyperlinks inside the message. Attackers use a variety of techniques to gain access to a target's email account such as spear-phishing, social engineering, and malware. Once they have access, they can monitor the account and learn about the target's business practices including who they communicate with and how they conduct financial transactions. This knowledge allows the attacker to create convincing emails that appear to be from a trusted source and request the victim to perform a specific action such as transferring funds to a fraudulent account.

It's important to note that BEC attacks are not as simple as just avoiding emails from people you don't know. Attackers can compromise the accounts of people you do know, and their emails may appear to be legitimate. This is why it's crucial to be vigilant and verify any requests for financial or sensitive information, especially if they seem unusual or urgent. It's also important to have strong security measures in place, such as two-factor authentication, to reduce the likelihood of unauthorized access to your email accounts. By staying aware and taking proactive steps to protect your email accounts, you can reduce your risk of falling victim to a BEC attack and potentially other more sophisticated attacks.

## Ransomware

Speaking of sophisticated attacks, ransomware has become one of the most prevalent and damaging types of cyber-attacks in recent years and it also looks quite different today from how it used to look. Ransomware version 1.0 meant that the attackers used encryption to lock up the victim's data, demanding payment in exchange for the decryption key. While having a backup of your data is important for recovery from a ransomware attack, it's not enough in the case of ransomware v2.

As if ransomware wasn't bad enough, attackers gave it quite an overhaul. Ransomware v2 takes the threat to a new level. Instead of just encrypting the victim's data, the attackers now steal sensitive data before encrypting it. They then threaten to release the data if the victim doesn't pay the ransom. This means that even if you have a backup of your data, the attacker still has your sensitive information and can use it for nefarious purposes. This leaves the attacker with the ability to accurately follow through on their threats to release your stolen data should their demands not be met with a ransom payment.

The attackers use sophisticated tactics to ensure that they have a copy of the victim's data before encrypting it. They may use remote access tools to gain access to the victim's network or use phishing emails to trick employees into downloading malware. Once they have access, they will spend weeks or even months observing the victim's network and exfiltrating sensitive data, giving the threat actors the upper hand. The attackers then have the victim's sensitive data, and they know that it's essential for the victim's business operations. This gives them leverage to demand a higher ransom than in a traditional ransomware attack. Even worse, there's no guarantee that the attacker will release the data even if the ransom is paid.

Unfortunately, ransomware is not going anywhere. According to the Cyber security and Infrastructure Security Agency (CISA), the average ransomware payment has increased by 311% in the last year. These specific types of attacks can be especially devastating for small and micro businesses that lack the resources to recover from such an attack. This is known as ransomware v2.0 and is becoming increasingly common. The potential fallout from such an attack can be catastrophic for businesses, leading to severe reputational damage and financial losses.

## Session Hijacks

Session token hijacking is also on the rise. Session hijacking is a type of cyber-attack that involves taking control of a user's session on a website or application without their knowledge or consent. This type of attack is relatively easy to execute and can be highly effective. A session hijack occurs when an attacker intercepts the user's session ID, a unique identifier that's used to authenticate the user's session, and then uses that ID to take control of the session. These attacks can give attackers access to sensitive data, including login credentials, banking information, and other personal data. One of the reasons session hijack attacks are so effective is that they can be difficult to detect. The user may not even realize that their session has been hijacked as the attacker can continue to use the session ID to access the user's account and carry out unauthorized activities. Additionally, session hijack attacks can be difficult to prevent as they can be carried out using a variety of techniques including man-in-the-middle attacks, cross-site scripting (XSS), or sniffing attacks. Case in point, a successful attack can be carried out by having the user simply click a link to a website, effectively capturing their session token after they've logged in. Because the user never leaves the official website of the software, file-sharing, or email service they use, it is almost impossible to detect. The ease with which these attacks can be carried out means that small businesses and their staff must take immediate and proactive steps to protect themselves.

## MITM

A MITM, or a Man-In-The-Middle, attack is a type of cyber-attack that involves intercepting communication between two parties and stealing or manipulating data. In this attack, the attacker positions themselves between the two parties, intercepts the communication, and then relays the data back and forth between the two parties without their knowledge. This can allow the attacker to steal sensitive information such as login credentials or financial data or manipulate the communication to carry out fraudulent activities. These attacks are also especially dangerous, as are BEC attacks, because they can be carried out without the victim's knowledge, making it exceptionally difficult to detect and prevent. Consequently speaking, they can be highly effective as the attacker can intercept data and manipulate it in real-time, allowing them to carry out fraudulent activities quickly and efficiently.

## Fileless Malware

Fileless malware is a growing threat that can have catastrophic effects on a business if left undetected. Unlike traditional malware, fileless malware does not rely on malicious files or software, making it virtually undetectable by traditional security solutions. Instead, it infects legitimate system processes, such as PowerShell or Windows Management Instrumentation (WMI), and uses them to carry out its malicious activities. This makes it incredibly difficult to detect and remove, leaving businesses vulnerable to significant data breaches, financial losses, and reputational damage.

Without proper zero trust security and AI XDR (eXtended Detection and Response) in place, businesses are at high risk of falling victim to fileless malware attacks. Attackers can use fileless malware to steal sensitive data, compromise systems, and carry out fraudulent activities, all without leaving any traceable evidence. Once a business has been infected, it can be extremely difficult and costly to remediate, often requiring the assistance of cyber security experts and significant downtime to fully remove the malware from the system.

The consequences of a fileless malware attack can be catastrophic, leading to financial losses, data breaches, and reputational damage that can take years to recover from. As such, it is crucial for businesses to take proactive measures to protect against this growing threat.

Overall, the above attacks are increasingly prevalent and highly effective, making them a significant threat to businesses of all sizes. While there are measures that businesses can take to mitigate these risks, it can be challenging, if not impossible without a dedicated cyber security team in the mix.

Without the necessary knowledge and resources, small businesses will struggle to identify the signs of a cyber-attack, leaving them vulnerable to potentially devastating consequences. This highlights the importance of investing in cyber security measures and working with experienced professionals who can help identify and mitigate potential vulnerabilities. By prioritizing cyber security and seeking assistance when necessary, businesses can better protect themselves from the damaging effects of cyber-attacks.

## The Targeting of Small Businesses

The threat of cyber-attacks on businesses is real and growing. Small businesses are particularly vulnerable and must take proactive steps to protect themselves because they are often seen as low-hanging fruit by attackers. Attackers know that many small businesses lack the resources and expertise to implement comprehensive cyber security measures, making them much more vulnerable to attacks.

According to a study by Verizon, 43% of all cyber-attacks target small businesses. With attackers becoming more sophisticated, it's becoming increasingly clear that small businesses must take every step available to properly protect themselves because not doing so comes at a very heavy price. The overall cost of a data breach can be significant with many small businesses unable to recover from such an event. Therefore, it's important for small businesses to take cyber security seriously and to invest in the necessary resources to protect themselves.

While many small businesses have IT personnel, regular IT teams may lack the experience and expertise required to keep up with the ever-changing threat landscape. This is where an outsourced cyber security service is a must. A specialized cyber security IT team can provide businesses with a much more proactive approach to cyber security, working with them to identify and address potential vulnerabilities before they are exploited. Instead of waiting for an attack to occur, these teams can identify these vulnerabilities and take steps to address them before an attack occurs. These teams can provide a very wide range of services including ongoing support and maintenance, risk assessments, vulnerability testing, implement-tation of advanced security controls, and cyber security training for employees, just to name a few.

Partnering with a trusted cyber security and IT services team can significantly reduce the risk of a cyber security breach and provide businesses with greater peace of mind. Cyber security is not a one-time event; it requires ongoing vigilance and attention to detail, so by partnering with a cyber security team, the business empowers themselves with the expertise and support they need to generate awareness and better protect themselves from cyber security threats — often times for an affordable monthly line item in their budget and a fraction cheaper than hiring a W2 employee.

## Respond or Fall Victim

Things have changed. Business as usual is no longer an option. Real-world scenarios have shown the devastating effects of a cyber-attack on small businesses. The costs associated with a cyber-attack can be significant and can lead to the loss of customers, reputation damage, and even bankruptcy.

As cyber-attacks become more advanced, businesses need to deploy advanced security measures to protect their data. Traditional antivirus and anti-malware systems are no longer sufficient to protect against modern attacks. Attackers can easily evade these systems by recompiling and rewriting software using AI, making detection extremely challenging.

It is crucial to recognize the importance of cyber security and take proactive steps to protect your business. It is also important to note that cyber security is not a one-time fix, but an ongoing process that requires continuous monitoring and improvement. Small business owners may think they can handle their cyber security needs on their own or delegate it to someone within their organization who may not have the expertise necessary to protect their business effectively. However, this can be a costly mistake.

A lack of specialized knowledge and expertise in cyber security can lead to an inadequate security infrastructure, leaving small businesses vulnerable to attacks. Small business owners may not have the resources to invest in advanced security technologies or stay up to date with the latest security trends and threats. This is a nightmare waiting to happen because, as a small business owner, you have a responsibility to protect your business from cyber-attacks, and the first step is to acknowledge the inevitability of being targeted.

Moreover, this means adopting multiple authentication requirements, strong access controls, and a zero-trust framework where all users, devices, and applications are treated as untrusted until proven otherwise. This also means investing in advanced XDR solutions affording the business AI-based Extended Detection and Response (XDR) solutions which can detect and respond to attacks in real-time. This includes adopting a zero-trust framework, investing in advanced XDR solutions, hiring a dedicated cyber security IT team, and having an incident response plan in place.

Businesses should also seriously consider hiring a dedicated cyber security IT team to proactively secure their systems and meet with them regularly to discuss new findings and upcoming IT strategy planning. In addition, all businesses must have an incident response plan in place, specifically outlining what to do and in what order in the event of a negative cyber incident. Since such an event is deemed as unavoidable with how things have changed, the business should also protect themselves with cyber insurance. Cyber insurance can provide financial protection in case of a breach, covering the cost of remediation, legal fees, and reputational damage. However, it is worth noting that most insurers will only provide coverage if the business can demonstrate that they have implemented robust security measures.

By taking these steps, businesses can minimize the risk of a breach, minimize the damage in case of an attack, and ensure that they are protected from financial and reputational loss. Remember, without these items in place, it's not a matter of if you get breached, but when. So, take action now to protect your business before it's too late.

## Conclusion

If you're a small business owner, you might think that having an IT department or an IT person is enough to protect your company from cyber threats, and that it might be overkill to invest in a full cyber security team. Unfortunately, that's not the case and couldn't be further from the gravity of the situation. The truth is that the risks associated with cyber-crime are simply too great to ignore by not putting a necessary team in place. The cost of a data breach can be significant with many small businesses unable to recover from such an event. Likewise, regular IT companies often lack the experience, expertise, and resources to adequately defend against today's advanced threat landscape. The reality is that businesses need specialized cyber security teams to help them stay ahead of the curve and protect their data. Therefore, investing in a specialized cyber security IT team is not just a smart business decision, but it's also essential for the long-term success of your business.

We believe that every business, regardless of size or industry, deserves the highest level of protection against cyber-crime. We are committed to helping small businesses like yours stay ahead of the curve and proactively protect themselves from cyber security threats. We have the expertise and experience to help businesses protect themselves from those cyber threats. We specialize in providing advanced XDR solutions, Zero Trust frameworks, and cyber security risk assessments that can help businesses identify vulnerabilities and develop effective strategies to defend against cyber-attacks. So, if you're looking for a trusted partner in cyber security and want to ensure your business is protected against cyber threats, don't wait. Our team of experts is here to help you identify potential vulnerabilities, provide ongoing support and training, and implement cutting-edge cyber security solutions to keep your business safe. Let us help you take the necessary steps to protect your business from cyber-crime, so you can focus on what you do best – running and growing your business.

Contact Sabre today to learn more about our services and how we can help you. As a special incentive, we're offering $500 off a Cyber security Risk Assessment for those who act fast and to thank you for reading this chapter. To take advantage of this offer, visit our website at: https://bookpromo.sabrecybersecurity.com.

Don't wait until it's too late. Protect your business today against the zero-day threats of tomorrow.

# About the Author

Jake McCann started with computers at a very young age. He tore his parents' computer apart and rebuilt it when he was just 8 years old, prompting them to purchase Jake his own system.

He spent countless hours trialing, testing, and researching all things technology. In High School Jake even started his own technology company specializing in Computer Repair.

Years later, the company grew to accommodate many computing and project needs for small businesses throughout Central Ohio. Today, Sabre specializes in full-service IT solutions, Cyber security risk mitigation, helpdesk services, technical consulting/design projects, and ongoing technology and cyber security management services for small businesses nationwide.

In addition to ongoing IT management and security for businesses, Sabre also regularly performs one-time projects like Email migration services, Workstation and Server hardware procurement and replacement, secure work from home implementation for staff, firewall and routing appliance installation, computer repair and network services, wireless access point setups and installation and data backup or restoration services. Sabre acts as an arm (with a Cyber security specialty) to an already existing business IT Department OR a supplement to that organization's IT person altogether. Sabre technicians work alongside the business owner and their staff closely to accomplish their technology and security goals. Sabre's mission is to grow business revenue through technology, freeing the business owner up to focus on what matters so they can get back to working 'on' their business and not just 'in' it. Sabre is currently managing hundreds of endpoint systems and looking to bring on new clients in the professional services industries.

# 5 Ways Your Business Can Reduce Cyber Risk

**By Nick D'Emanuele**

Let's make something clear: you are at risk of a cyber security attack.

The amount of risk you have and the success of an attack against your business will depend on how well you prepare before it happens. The sooner you accept this and take action, the better your chances of avoiding an attack and limiting the impact a successful attack can have on your business.

My goal in this chapter is to educate you about cyber security attacks and to give you some steps you can take to reduce your overall cyber risk.

## What is Cyber Risk?

Cyber risk is a measure of the chance your business will fall victim to a cyber security attack.

We are all at risk, but those who prepare – by educating themselves and their staff, by putting appropriate security measures in place, and by planning for recovery and business continuity in the aftermath of an attack – have the lowest risk.

Some examples of risky behaviors include running old operating systems or software versions that are no longer supported by the vendor. Or not having a proper backup strategy in place, or re-using passwords on several different accounts. Other examples include not providing training to help keep your staff informed of the types of threats that exist, how to identify malicious activity in your organization, and what to do when that type of activity is encountered.

Some other risky behaviors that may not be as obvious include not limiting employee access to the essential functions and data they need to perform their jobs, not keeping business bank accounts separated, and not monitoring for signs of data breach or exposure.

## What is a Cyber Security Attack?

A cyber security attack – one of the biggest risks business owners face today – is when an unauthorized individual or organization – a threat actor – disrupts business by gaining access to sensitive information or services that are used by or protected by the business in some way.

This could be in the form of gaining access to business accounts and stealing data, stealing or redirecting money, deleting or encrypting files, or shutting down or locking up systems. Sometimes these attacks can be for financial gain, but they can also be to simply wreak havoc on a business for the fun of it. Sometimes, the attacks are used to stage even larger hits against a business's vendors, customers, or associates as well.

For those in the know, the threat of a cyber security attack can (and should) bring about a sense of fear. A fear of data loss, spoiled reputation, loss of money, and a fear of losing the business entirely. For others, the threat of a cyber security attack may mean nothing at all because of the false belief that they aren't big enough to be a target or a victim of an attack, or that they do business entirely in the cloud so there is no risk to their business. Unfortunately, this is a dangerous position to have.

The truth is, a cyber security attack can and likely will occur if you don't take conscious action to protect yourself.

## How are Cyber Security Attacks Changing?

When we consider a cyber security attack, we commonly think about trying to open a file and being faced with a message that you have been hacked, and you need to pay a bitcoin ransom to an anonymous wallet to get your files back.

No problem – you're smart and prepared, so instead of paying the ransom, you'll just rebuild your systems and restore your files. Threat mitigated, right? The reality is that although you may be able to recover your files from a backup, there is a lot more to consider if you've been the victim of an attack.

Today, it's very likely that a ransom attack is the last step in a longer hacking campaign that has already been in play for weeks or months on your systems, after the hacker already has everything that they need from you.

In the wake of an attack, you now must consider additional possibilities such as could the attacker still be in your system, and will they strike again? What data was compromised before the files were encrypted? Do they have access to other information such as sensitive client data, passwords, bank accounts, secret keys, and other information that will enable additional attacks against your business in the future?

We must also consider reporting cyber security attacks to the proper authorities. Many new laws have been created in response to the rise in attacks to help keep the public informed about breaches that occur, how they occur, and what has been compromised.

## Why do Cyber Security Attacks Keep Happening?

Over time, the methods that hackers use to compromise their victims change by leveraging new vulnerabilities, streamlining their processes, and taking advantage of new tools such as AI to increase their chances of success.

Consider the following:

Vulnerabilities in operating systems and software are discovered every day, and many times only discovered after the hackers have already found and are actively exploiting them.

Hacking organizations are now operating as larger companies, developing tools and best practices to continually adjust their methods and targets over time, improving their success rates.

Threat actors are reaching out to employees of companies they are targeting, paying large sums of money in exchange for access to the client systems, enabling attacks.

The rise and popularity of new AI tools give hackers the ability to create content that appears legitimate, making it easier to trick users into performing actions that will facilitate an attack.

Deepfake video technology can create false videos of people doing and saying things that can lead to falling victim to a scam.

Platforms such as dating websites, job hunting sites, and other social media platforms are being used to build trust with victims and then put them into sensitive or compromising positions where the only thing they believe is keeping them safe is a payout to those who have put them into this position.

These are just some of the ways threat actors continue to get footholds into businesses. It doesn't mean you will necessarily fall victim to these methods, but you don't know where the next attack is going to come from, so you need to be ready, and you need to make sure your staff is ready and knows how to respond (not react!) when they encounter these new scenarios.

## Business Owners Face a Lot of Risk

Business owners face an immense amount of risk. The risk of not having enough funds to make it work; the risk of not having enough time to have a life outside of the business; the risk of not being successful.

But that's why we do it, right? Without the risk, where is the reward? Maybe your reward is to be your own boss or to make lots of money. Or maybe it's to have a flexible schedule or to service a specific group of people, or to bring a needed product to market.

One risk that cannot be ignored is the risk of a cyber security attack. These attacks don't just happen to the large, big box companies out there. They are happening to businesses of all sizes in increasing frequency and cost to the businesses that are attacked.

These attacks can play out in many ways, but the end results carry huge risks such as:

## Encrypted Files

This is when the files that contain your important data are scrambled and unusable. It's typically part of a ransomware attack where a threat actor will offer a code to unscramble your files in exchange for money.

## Inaccessible Systems

Some cyber security attacks are so destructive that the systems you depend on are unavailable for use due to corruption or deletion to the point they are not usable.

## Leaked Data

Many attacks today start with an export of all the sensitive data that can be found on a compromised system or network. Hackers will then either use this information to perform additional attacks or request a ransom payment to prevent exposing this sensitive data to the dark web where other threat actors can use it for malicious purposes.

## Stolen Money

A very popular attack today is the Business Email Compromise (BEC) where hackers get a foothold in a company email system, watch the communications between a business and their clients and vendors, and look for a high value business transaction with the hopes of impersonating the business just before the exchange of money and then redirecting funds to a fake account.

## Closed Business

In some cases, the cost of recovery or the loss of business due to ruined reputation or relationships is enough to force the business to close. This is an unfortunate result that can occur when the attack disrupts business to the point that it is impossible to recover.

These outcomes all start with threat actors getting into your systems or accessing your private data in some way such as an email system compromise, unauthorized programs running on computers, or accounts being accessed by unauthorized users.

In many cases, simple actions performed ahead of time can prevent these outcomes. The problem is that most business owners don't realize how easy it is to minimize the risk of a cyber security attack by following a few best practice guidelines I'll share with you here.

## 5 Ways Your Business Can Reduce Cyber Risk

While there is no guaranteed way to 100% avoid a cyber security attack, there are some things you can do to help minimize your risk of falling victim to an attack and to minimize the damage suffered by your business and reputation (and wallet) in the wake of an attack.

### Enable Multi-Factor Authentication (MFA)

Enabling Multi-Factor Authentication (MFA) on all your accounts is one of the easiest things you can do to reduce your cyber risk to protect your business.

Multi-factor authentication is a method of securing your accounts by using more than one form of identification. Typically, this will be a combination of something you know, such as a password or passphrase, and something you have, such as a phone number, an email account, or a physical token with a rotating code that must be entered after the password is accepted.

While we always recommend using strong, unique passwords on all your accounts, the point of MFA is that, even if someone were to get your password (through a guess, a hack, or another compromised service that you use) the person logging in would still need access to something physical that you own to get access to your account.

While multi-factor authentication is not guaranteed protection – there are cases where it has been bypassed by a dedicated hacker – it can greatly reduce your risk of compromise.

Please enable MFA on ALL your accounts, not just your business accounts. Consider a scenario where your protected business account lists a personal, unprotected email account for recovery purposes. A compromised personal account without MFA is one way a hacker can still get into a protected business account.

**Keep System Software Updated**

Many times, hackers gain access by using unpatched vulnerabilities in a targeted system. This is completely avoidable by making sure you're applying updates when they become available and always running current versions of software.

This is usually a simple task for business owners because you are likely prompted to perform updates on a regular basis by your devices and vendors. But it's easy to pause the updates, put them off, or decide not to do them because of compatibility, cost, or other issues. But delaying these updates could have disastrous results for your business.

Keeping systems up to date is more than just applying updates to your operating system. It's also making sure to apply updates to the software you use every day and upgrading the software when it's no longer receiving support from the vendor. Most vendors only provide security updates for software for a certain amount of time. That copy of Word 2010 might still work, but that doesn't mean it's safe to use. That old iron in the closet with the frayed power cord might work, but one of these days it will cause a fire.

While zero-day threats do exist (vulnerabilities in software that are being exploited by hackers before a vendor can release a patch), the likelihood of being compromised by an unpatched vulnerability that has been around for a while with fixes available is a lot greater than being the victim of a new vulnerability just recently detected. Keeping systems patched will reduce your cyber risk.

### Provide Security Awareness Training

Adopting a culture of security within your organization will help strengthen your business against falling victim to a cyber security attack. Providing cyber security awareness training is a great way to do this.

The right training program will provide weekly, monthly, and yearly reminders of the methods hackers use to compromise businesses, what to look for in emails to verify their legitimacy, and what to do when faced with a situation that seems suspicious. It will also provide metrics about who has completed the training as well as provide testing scenarios such as phishing emails to users to see who may need additional training.

Another way to keep security front of mind is to hang situational posters as reminders to be on the lookout for suspicious activity and to always think about how the decisions you make in every situation can impact the overall security of your organization.

Keeping a culture of security within your organization helps keep everybody alert and helps them make the right choices to help avoid an attack, thereby reducing your overall cyber risk.

### Limit Access to Computer Systems and Data

One thing that's often overlooked in many businesses is limiting access to systems and data that is not needed by users to do their job.

Many times, users are configured to have full administrative rights on their devices which gives them access to do literally anything they want on their system. This doesn't necessarily mean they will intentionally do something malicious, but it sets the stage for users to install unauthorized programs that can lead to a cyber security attack against a business.

This is especially damaging when users have uncontrolled access to files and systems on the business network that they don't need to do their job. A cyber security attacker will have free reign to access anything the user has access to, greatly increasing the damage that can be done during an attack.

When access is controlled – limited to the functions each user needs and nothing more – a compromised user will still wreak havoc on a business network, but the damage will be contained to what the affected user has access to rather than the entire company's systems and data.

A best practice for user access is to provide non-administrative use of their own devices and specific, directed access to only the systems and data needed to perform their job and no more.

This will help to limit the cyber risk of your business a great deal.

## Implement Proper Backups

While a good backup system won't prevent an attack, it can improve the chances of recovery if files are deleted, encrypted, or otherwise inaccessible following a successful cyber security attack. A proper backup will be automated, air-gapped, and distributed among multiple locations.

Automated backups run on a regular basis without user interaction. In a typical organization, this can be real-time backups as data changes, periodic backups throughout the day, and then daily backups to capture end-of-day changes. Relying on connecting backup drives and running backups manually will almost always lead to missed backups and loss of data in a cyber security attack scenario.

Air-gapped backups create a physical or logical "gap" between your active files and your backups so that a hacker is not able to delete or destroy the files you may need to recover your systems. This means that the USB drive that always stays connected to your computer is NOT an air-gapped solution, and while it may save you from accidental file deletion, it will be useless in recovering a compromised and encrypted file system.

Distributed backups ensure that copies of your files exist in multiple locations. Typically, this would be locally in production; backed up to an onsite appliance; and replicated to another location or cloud service for safe keeping.

Be mindful of backing up critical business data in cloud-based systems.  Many vendors give you an option to backup or download your data locally. This can be a great way to keep a copy of the data separate from your cloud-based system in case it is breached, offline, or otherwise inaccessible for an extended amount of time.

## Conclusion

These are just a few of the many things you can do to improve your security and reduce your cyber risk. We recommend hiring a professional, cyber security-focused IT company that can offer a variety of additional services in a layered approach to help reduce your risk further and to help minimize your downtime if you ever fall victim to a cyber security attack.

Please understand there is no silver bullet when it comes to preventing cyber security attacks. Nobody can guarantee your safety because there are simply too many variables and too many things changing every single day. You must first accept that there is risk, and then implement what you can control to help minimize it.

Putting systems in place to minimize the risk of an attack and to minimize the downtime experienced in the wake of an attack will give your business the best chances of survival against this growing threat.

# About the Author

Nick D'Emanuele is the Founder and President of Endecom IT, a cyber security-focused IT services company based in Hartford, Connecticut.

With over 25 years of experience with computers, networks, and cyber security, Nick is committed to making technology easy to use by providing expert solutions backed by a highly personable customer service experience.

Founded in 2005, Endecom IT started as a break-fix computer support company providing as-needed IT support to local businesses. Since then, it has grown into a full-service proactive Managed Services Provider (MSP) supporting businesses of all sizes, and today focuses on providing highly effective cyber security solutions.

To learn more about how Endecom IT can provide highly effective solutions for your business, backed by a customer service experience you will absolutely love, please visit https://endecom.com, call (860) 266-7900, or e-mail Nick directly at nick@endecom.com.

# The Cyber Security Guide: 5 Things Your Business NEEDS Now

**By Mike Bloomfield**

In today's digital landscape, larger corporations face an ever-increasing threat of cyber-attacks. With more sophisticated methods employed by cybercriminals, it has become vital for organizations to bolster their cyber security measures. This chapter targets larger corporations with IT departments, highlighting the importance of partnering with a Managed Service Provider (MSP) to help implement co-managed IT solutions. We will cover five essential cyber security measures that can significantly enhance your organization's security posture and protect valuable data.

## Section 1: The Importance of Employee Training

No matter the size of a corporation, employees can be the weakest link in cyber security. Educating employees on identifying and responding to potential cyber threats such as phishing emails and social engineering scams is crucial. According to a report by Proofpoint, 99% of cyber-attacks rely on human interaction, highlighting the importance of employee awareness in mitigating cyber risks.

### 1.1 Employee Training and Security Culture

Creating a security-aware culture within your organization is crucial for long-term cyber security success. By fostering an environment where employees understand the importance of their role in safeguarding the organization's data, you can significantly reduce the risks associated with human error and insider threats. A strong security culture encourages employees to report potential threats and take an active role in protecting the organization.

### 1.2 Tailored Training Programs

Partnering with an MSP allows access to expert-designed training programs that are tailored to your organization's specific needs. These programs can cover various topics, including password management, safe internet browsing habits, and recognizing phishing attempts. MSPs can also provide ongoing training updates, ensuring that employees stay informed about the latest threats and best practices.

## Section 2: Two-Factor Authentication

Implementing two-factor authentication (2FA) adds an extra layer of security to user accounts, reducing the likelihood of unauthorized access. In 2019, Microsoft reported that 2FA could have prevented 99.9% of account compromise attacks. Working with an MSP ensures the proper deployment of 2FA solutions, offering a more secure environment than relying on passwords alone.

### 2.1 Types of Two-Factor Authentication

There are various types of 2FA, including SMS-based codes, authenticator apps, and hardware tokens. Each method has its advantages and potential drawbacks. An MSP can help your organization select the most appropriate 2FA method for your needs, ensuring a balance between security and usability.

### 2.2 Implementing 2FA Across the Organization

It is essential to apply 2FA not only to employee accounts but also to other critical systems such as remote access portals, VPNs, and cloud services. An MSP can help your organization identify which systems require 2FA and assist in the implementation process.

## Section 3: Network Segmentation

Network segmentation involves dividing a network into smaller subnetworks to improve security and reduce the potential impact of a cyberattack. Implementing network segmentation can limit the spread of malware and reduce the likelihood of a successful attack. A 2017 report by Verizon found that 81% of hacking-related breaches leveraged stolen or weak passwords, many of which could have been prevented through proper network segmentation. Partnering with an MSP can help your organization implement effective network segmentation, providing an additional layer of protection.

### 3.1 Benefits of Network Segmentation

In addition to increased security, network segmentation can improve network performance and simplify regulatory compliance. By separating sensitive data from less critical systems, organizations can more easily manage access controls and implement security policies.

### 3.2 Network Segmentation Best Practices

When implementing network segmentation, it is important to follow best practices, such as conducting a thorough risk assessment, creating clear security policies, and regularly monitoring network traffic. An MSP can help guide your organization through these steps, ensuring the successful implementation of network segmentation.

## Section 4: Regular Software Updates

Maintaining up-to-date software and operating systems is critical for the security of your organization's IT systems. Regular updates patch known vulnerabilities and reduce the risk of a successful cyberattack. The 2017 WannaCry ransomware attack affected over 200,000 computers across 150 countries, largely due to outdated systems. MSPs can manage software updates and ensure your systems are always up to date, safeguarding your organization against potential threats.

### 4.1 The Risks of Outdated Software

Outdated software can expose your organization to a variety of threats, including data breaches, ransomware, and malware infections. Cybercriminals often target known vulnerabilities in older software versions, making it crucial to stay current with updates.

### 4.2 Centralized Patch Management

MSPs can help your organization establish a centralized patch management process, ensuring that all devices and software are consistently updated. By working with an MSP, you can automate the update process, reducing the risk of human error and ensuring that patches are applied promptly.

## Section 5: Data Backup and Recovery

Having a reliable data backup and recovery plan is crucial in the event of a cyber-attack or other disaster. Regularly backing up data and testing the recovery process can make the difference between recovering quickly and suffering significant losses. According to a study by the Ponemon Institute, the average cost of a data breach in 2021 was $ 4.24 million, a 10% increase compared to the previous year. Partnering with an MSP can help your organization implement robust backup and recovery solutions, minimizing potential damages and ensuring business continuity in the face of a cyber-attack.

### 5.1 The Importance of Regular Data Backups

Data backups should be performed regularly to minimize data loss in the event of a cyber-attack or system failure. An MSP can help your organization determine the optimal backup frequency based on your data needs and risk tolerance.

## 5.2 Offsite and Cloud-Based Backup Solutions

Offsite and cloud-based backup solutions provide additional layers of protection by storing backup data in remote locations. This ensures that your organization can recover its data even if onsite backups are compromised. MSPs can help you implement secure offsite and cloud-based backup solutions, ensuring the safety and availability of your data.

## 5.3 Testing and Validation

Regular testing and validation of backup and recovery processes are essential to ensure that your organization can quickly and effectively restore its operations in the event of a disaster. MSPs can conduct periodic tests to verify the integrity of your backups and the effectiveness of your recovery plans.

In summary, larger corporations with IT departments must recognize the value of partnering with a Managed IT Service Provider for co-managed IT services. By collaborating with an MSP, organizations can benefit from expertly designed security services, help desk overflow, and tailored solutions to enhance their cyber security posture. Implementing the five essential cyber security measures discussed in this chapter – employee training, two-factor authentication, network segmentation, regular software updates, and data backup and recovery – can significantly reduce the risk of a cyberattack and protect your organization's valuable data.

IT department heads should proactively seek partnerships with MSPs, leveraging their expertise and resources to maintain strong cyber security measures and ensure the safety and success of their organizations in an increasingly complex digital landscape. By investing in cyber security and working with an MSP, corporations can stay ahead of emerging threats, safeguard their valuable data and assets, and maintain their competitive edge in the market.

Remember, cyber security is not a one-time project, but an ongoing process that requires constant attention, monitoring, and adaptation. By partnering with a trusted MSP and implementing these five essential cyber security measures, your organization can significantly enhance its security posture, minimize risks, and ensure a more secure future in the ever-changing world of cyber threats.

## Cyber Security Best Practices

In addition to the five essential cyber security measures discussed, here are some additional best practices to help further secure your organization's digital landscape.

**Vulnerability Management:** Regularly conduct vulnerability assessments and penetration tests to identify and remediate potential security weaknesses in your organization's IT infrastructure. A managed IT service provider can help you develop a comprehensive vulnerability management program to proactively address potential threats and minimize risk exposure.

**Incident Response Planning:** Establish a well-defined incident response plan to guide your organization's actions in the event of a cyber-attack or security breach. Ensure all employees are aware of their roles and responsibilities in responding to incidents. Collaborate with your MSP to develop and implement a robust incident response plan that meets your organization's unique needs and requirements.

**Security Awareness Campaigns:** Develop and maintain an ongoing security awareness campaign to educate employees about cyber security risks and best practices. Utilize a variety of communication channels, such as newsletters, intranet articles, and webinars to reinforce key messages and maintain employee engagement. Partnering with an MSP can provide access to a wealth of educational resources and expertise to support your security awareness efforts.

**Secure Configuration:** Ensure all systems and devices are configured according to security best practices and organizational policies. This includes configuring firewalls, routers, and other network devices, as well as implementing strong password policies and access controls. A managed IT service provider can assist with the development and enforcement of secure configuration standards, helping to reduce the risk of unauthorized access and data breaches.

**Monitoring and Logging:** Implement continuous monitoring and logging of your organization's network and IT systems to detect and respond to security events in real time. Work with your MSP to establish a centralized security information and event management (SIEM) solution that aggregates and analyzes log data from across your organization, enabling faster detection and response to potential threats.

**Encryption:** Protect sensitive data both at rest and in transit using strong encryption algorithms. This can help prevent unauthorized access to your organization's sensitive information in the event of a breach. An MSP can help you identify and deploy the most suitable encryption solutions for your organization's unique needs.

**Regular Security Audits:** Conduct regular security audits to assess your organization's compliance with industry standards and regulatory requirements. Security audits can help identify gaps in your cyber security posture and provide recommendations for improvement. Partnering with an MSP ensures that you have access to skilled security professionals who can conduct thorough security audits and provide actionable insights to enhance your organization's security.

**Insider Threat Management:** Develop a comprehensive insider threat management program to identify and mitigate the risk of data breaches or other malicious actions by employees or contractors. This should include background checks, role-based access controls, regular monitoring of user activity, and ongoing security training. Collaborating with an MSP can provide you with the necessary expertise and resources to create an effective insider threat management program tailored to your organization's specific needs.

**Patch Management:** Establish a robust patch management process to ensure timely identification and deployment of security patches for all software and hardware components within your organization. Unpatched systems can expose your organization to significant risks as attackers can easily exploit known vulnerabilities. An MSP can help streamline your patch management process, ensuring that all systems are up-to-date and protected against known threats.

**Disaster Recovery Planning:** Develop a comprehensive disaster recovery plan that outlines the steps your organization should take to recover from various types of disasters, including cyber-attacks, natural disasters, and equipment failures. Work with your MSP to create a disaster recovery plan that meets your organization's unique needs and requirements and regularly test the plan to ensure its effectiveness.

By implementing these additional best practices alongside the five essential cyber security measures discussed earlier, your organization can significantly improve its overall security posture. Partnering with a managed IT service provider for co-managed IT solutions offers numerous benefits, including access to expert security services, help desk overflow, and tailored solutions designed to meet your organization's unique needs and challenges.

In conclusion, large corporations with IT departments must recognize the importance of investing in robust cyber security measures and leveraging the expertise of managed IT service providers. By implementing a comprehensive, multi-layered approach to cyber security that includes employee training, two-factor authentication, network segmentation, regular software updates, data backup and recovery, vulnerability management, incident response planning, security awareness campaigns, secure configuration, monitoring and logging, encryption, regular security audits, insider threat management, patch management, and disaster recovery planning, your organization can significantly reduce the risk of cyber-attacks and protect valuable data.

IT department heads should take the initiative to establish and maintain strong partnerships with managed IT service providers. These partnerships can help organizations stay ahead of the perpetually shifting cyber security landscape, ensuring the safety and success of their businesses in an increasingly interconnected digital world.

As cyber threats continue to grow in complexity and sophistication, it is crucial for large corporations to stay vigilant and proactive in their cyber security efforts. By investing in co-managed IT solutions and working closely with managed IT service providers, organizations can tap into a wealth of knowledge, resources, and expertise that will enable them to maintain a strong security posture, ultimately safeguarding their assets, reputation, and long-term success.

# About the Author

Mike Bloomfield is the President of Tekie Geek, the IT Superheroes of Cyber security and a Managed Service Provider based in Staten Island, NY. Mike and his team of Geekvengers are dedicated to providing clients with top-notch IT services, including Managed IT Services, Co-Managed IT Services, Business Continuity, Cloud Computing, and Unified Communication.

With over two decades of experience in the industry, Mike has made a name for himself with his innovative solutions and expertise. He is an Amazon bestselling author, having published several books on IT security. His passion and knowledge in the industry have earned him a reputation as an IT expert and have led to his frequent invitation to sit on the advisory boards of several vendors, including Mailprotector, CryptoStopper, Cytracom, ThreatAdvice, and GetChanneled.

Under Mike's leadership, Tekie Geek has become one of the fastest-growing MSPs in Staten Island, winning several awards and recognition from the Staten Island Chamber of Commerce, SIEDC, and Channel Futures. With their core company values of Clients, Culture, and Community, the Geekvengers work tirelessly to protect their clients from the rising IT threats and to provide peace of mind.

When he's not working, Mike enjoys spending time with his family and is a fan of Marvel and Star Wars movies. He is also actively involved in the community and serves on several boards, including the Staten Island Chamber of Commerce, Meals on Wheels, and Staten Island Business Outreach Center.

"I have always had a passion for technology and a drive to stay at the forefront of advancements in the industry. My goal is to use my expertise to help businesses protect themselves from the ever-evolving IT threats and to provide peace of mind to clients. I believe in putting clients first, fostering a positive company culture, and giving back to the community."

## Business Awards

- Staten Island Chamber of Commerce Lou Miller Award

- SIEDC 20 Under 40 Award
- SIEDC Top 31 Businesses in Staten Island
- SIEDC Top 31 Fastest Growing Businesses in Staten Island
- Star Network King of Staten Island
- Star Network Power Duo of Staten Island
- Star Network Stars Under 40
- Channel Futures MSP 501
- Channel Futures NextGen 101

Organizations

- Board of Directors, Meals on Wheels of Staten Island
- Board of Directors, Treasurer, Staten Island Business Outreach Center
- Board of Directors, Staten Island Board of Realtors
- Board of Directors, Co-Chair, South Shore BID
- Board of Directors, Staten Island Chamber of Commerce
- Former Board of Directors, Gotham Trinity Initiative

- Past-President, The Executive Club of Staten Island
- Advisory Board, Mailprotector
- Advisory Board, Canauri
- Advisory Board, Cytracom
- Advisory Board, LendARR
- Former Advisory Board, ThreatAdvice
- Advisory Board, GetChanneled

Published Books

- *Hack Proof Your Business - Volume 2, Co-Author, Amazon Best Seller*
- *Stay Calm – How a Crisis Can Strengthen Your Business, Co-Author, Amazon Best Seller*
- *Why Your Business Must Have Cyber security Risk Assessments, Co-Author, Amazon Best Seller*
- *Cyber Attack Prevention, Co-Author, Amazon Best Seller*

## Contact Details

To schedule a consultation for your Business IT needs, please get in touch with us:

Website: https://www.tekiegeek.com

Client Testimonial Videos:
https://love.tekiegeek.com

Email: sales@tekiegeek.com

Facebook: https://facebook.com/tekiegeek

LinkedIn:
https://www.linkedin.com/in/mikebloomfield/

Phone: (347) 830-7322

# IT Negligence: The Secret Business Killer

**By Brett Gallant**

IT negligence, in the simplest of terms, is a failure to invest the time, money, and energy in the people and technological infrastructure that are needed to support, monitor, control, and protect the technology that is relevant to both SMBs and large corporations.

Negligence is a choice, a human one. Some people choose to ignore things day after day, week after week, and month after month. Human beings, as flawed as we are, make unhealthy choices all the time. We may choose to eat pizza over salad, watch TV instead of engaging our minds, or stay in jobs and relationships we've outgrown because we are either afraid of the unknown or simply unwilling to make a change because it seems like too much work.

In time, neglecting our bodies, minds, hearts (and businesses) can have devastating results. Obviously, it's easier to do nothing than to invest in the resources it takes to evolve. But the world is changing at breakneck speed, and if we neglect the things that are most important to us – the things that threaten our very existence – we are actively participating in our own demise.

Why are we intermingling personal choices with professional ones? Because IT negligence is not just a business topic. It's personnel.

There are a lot of stories in the news about the role that human error plays in cyber-attacks.

Take, for example, the cyber-attack on the Newfoundland and Labrador healthcare system in Canada.[1] The Hive Ransomware Group established a VPN connection and used the credentials of an employee to steal the personal records of more than 58,000 people. It is unknown whether they paid the ransom demand or if Hive went on to resell private information on the dark web.

While human error is a valid topic and ongoing cyber awareness training is a key component in cyber security, it's just the tip of the iceberg when it comes to IT negligence. It's the non-errors – the conscious decisions that SMBs make – that can kill a business.

---

[1] https://www.cbc.ca/news/canada/newfoundland-labrador/nl-cyberattack-explained-1.6781977

Why do we downplay the impact of human errors? Because they are accidents. Costly ones, but they are unplanned, unforeseen, uncalculated mistakes, and we believe that IT negligence is more intentional than that.

It may seem counter-intuitive to use "intentional," and "negligence" in the same sentence, but it's an accurate statement. We've done countless cyber security risk assessments over the years to identify internal and external threats. The reports clearly show security gaps that can expose company data to hackers and weaken system operations.

The information also shows how those weaknesses can result in financial loss and irreparable damage to businesses. And yet, many SMBs turn a blind eye to the fact-based data we provide and make the deliberate decision to do nothing about it.

For example, we recently did a cyber security review for a local business that has over 200 employees. The results were astonishing...in a bad way. Their only form of cyber security? Microsoft Defender, the anti-malware component of Microsoft Windows that was first released in 2006 and is now a basic building block in Windows 10 and 11.

Did the results of the cyber risk review serve as a wake-up call for them? Unfortunately not. They made no changes at all. If that's not cyber security negligence, what is?

## What is Slowly Killing Your SMB?

IT infrastructure is a complicated network of moving parts. It includes hardware, software, networks, servers, storage, backups, and, of course, people. Let's break down the top three: hardware, software, and backup and disaster recovery plans, into healthy, bite-sized morsels.

### Hardware

Old hardware – computers, tablets, cell phones, keyboards, monitors, printers scanners, IoT devices, etc. – can be a significant threat to cyber security. Many businesses delay upgrading their hardware, due to cost, until there are significant problems with their equipment. But by doing so, they may be setting themselves up for a major cyber-attack.

As software programs continue to develop, the minimum operational requirements for hardware systems increase. Meaning older hardware either becomes incapable of running newer programs, or software providers stop supporting older versions of their product.

You need look no further than Microsoft Windows to understand the ramifications of delaying an upgrade. In two separate excerpts from an article by Microsoft, they wrote:

"Support for Windows 7 ended on January 14, 2020, and Windows 8 went out of support on January 12, 2016. Devices running either version of Windows no longer receive security updates for the Office apps, including features, security, and other quality updates."

"Using Microsoft 365 on older, unsupported operating systems may cause performance and reliability issues over time. To maintain the reliability and stability of Microsoft 365, we strongly recommend you take advantage of the latest hardware capabilities by moving to a new PC with Windows 11."[2]

Additionally, some old hardware (not just computers, all hardware) can't support the latest cyber security measures like advanced encryption, biometric identification, and customizable passwords. For example, older IoT devices came with default passwords that users were unable to change. So that innocent-

---

[2] https://support.microsoft.com/en-au/office/what-windows-end-of-support-means-for-office-and-microsoft-365-34e28be4-1e4f-4928-b210-3f45d8215595

looking smartwatch can be a hacker's low-hanging fruit.

Let's not forget the personnel component when it comes to hardware. In the past, most employees used company hardware inside brick-and-mortar buildings. Now, with the advent of the hashtag movements such as #WFH (work from home), #BYOD (bring your own devices), and #IoT (the internet of things), cyber threats have increased exponentially in the past few years.

Bottom line, the cost of upgrading your hardware is significantly less than the price you'll pay by that old hardware failing. In addition to upgrading equipment every 3-5 years, it's imperative to have a policy and procedure plan in place for employees (non-compliance should have consequences) that addresses the cyber security parameters of using outdated personal devices to access company data.

## Software

We like to think of hardware as the body (or physical structure) of your IT infrastructure and software as the brain. The nice thing about software – beyond the programs that are pre-installed on computers – is that businesses get to choose the way their "brain" functions.

When most people think about software, the first thing that comes to mind are the programs they've chosen to run their businesses. These software apps – whether downloaded onto your computer or offered as a cloud solution – are part of a tech stack that includes (but isn't limited to): a CRM, communication platforms, productivity tools, etc.

But software is so much more far-reaching than that. The brain of your technology begins with the operating system, servers, and storage choices you make. After that, everything that "thinks for you," is software.

Some examples of the most popular software providers are Microsoft 365, Salesforce, Slack, WordPress, FreshBooks, Zoom, Paypal, Keeper, DocuSign, etc. There are also marketing tools like Zoho, Buffer, Canva, and Grammarly that are commonly used.

However, most people forget that search engines are software too. So every time you use Google as a search engine – or any Google Workspace apps like Gmail, Drive, and Docs – you're working with software applications.

As great (and necessary) as software is, it is also the leading cause of cyber security breaches. There is no other layer of your IT infrastructure that is a bigger liability. This is especially true when businesses continue to use old software programs because they have major vulnerabilities and unpatched components.

Remember, people are responsible for negligence – yes, that's another counter-intuitive phrase...responsible for negligence – and hackers are counting on slackers.

So, what does software negligence mean? The shortlist is three things: ignoring software updates, refusing to invest in a cyber security stack, and disregarding cyber awareness training. Yes, we know that people are not software, but they interact with software. Let's take a closer look at each of these.

**Software Updates** are released for two reasons: to introduce new features or to patch security vulnerabilities. Zero-day attacks happen between the time a vulnerability is discovered but not yet patched. When cyber-criminals hear about these security gaps, they race to cash in on them. If users don't update their systems as soon as they are notified (including Google updates and app alerts on cell phones), that's blatant IT negligence.

**Cyber Security Stacks** include a multitude of security layers. It's imperative that SMBs invest in software tools that go beyond a basic firewall and virus protection. Businesses need software that provides encryption, multi-factor authentication, automated/redundant/multi-locational backups, backup failure monitoring, anti-phishing/spam/malware protection, data breach monitoring, etc. SMBs also need to have a browser manager and cleaner, a VPN, AdBlock tools, adware protection, virus removal software, and ransomware protection. Failing to invest in a comprehensive cyber stack is IT negligence.

**Cyber Awareness Training** is a key component in cyber security. The cyber landscape is constantly changing, so ongoing training is imperative, and team members must be tested to ensure they are threat ready. Cyber awareness training should address topics such as phishing attacks, removable media threats, passwords, 2FA, physical security, mobile device security, remote work safety, public Wi-Fi usage, cloud security, social media use, internet and email threats, social engineering tactics, off-premises security, and the importance of installing software updates. If you don't have ongoing training for employees, you're guilty of IT negligence.

## Backups and Disaster Recovery

If hardware is the body and software is the brain, then company data is the heart and soul of your business. Data breaches, cyber-attacks, and equipment failures are just some of the potential catastrophes that can kill your business. Without robust backup solutions (notice that's plural) and a detailed disaster recovery plan in place, you are at risk of losing business-critical data.

### Backups

Ultimately, backups should happen in real-time. Automated backups should also be redundant and stored in multiple locations. There are many options when it comes to data storage – On-premises, HDD, SSD/Flash storage, hybrid storage, cloud storage, hybrid cloud storage, etc. – so it's important to do your homework when choosing the best option(s) for your business.

In general, we don't recommend storing business data on hardware that can break down, get lost or stolen, or have limited storage capacity. Here's an example of why....

We had a former non-profit client who was having issues with their server. When fixing the situation, I noticed that his existing backup drives were getting old. I told him to replace them, but I knew he was slow to implement change, so I decided to put an additional backup solution in place as a precautionary measure.

He eventually put the new drivers in place but never checked to be sure the configuration was correct. When the server crashed three months later, I checked the new drivers; no data had been stored. Fortunately, the backup drive that I put in place was still backing up nightly. If it hadn't, all of his business data would have been gone completely.

However, a single, on-premises storage solution is not what we recommend. That, in itself, is IT negligence. Cloud storage solutions backup information in real-time, and the data is stored in multiple geo-locations. It is also scalable, affordable, and can be accessed from anywhere in the world; provided you have an internet location.

However, highly regulated data that is subject to strict archiving and replication requirements are usually better suited to a private cloud environment. Less sensitive data can be stored in the public cloud. Some organizations use hybrid clouds to supplement their internal storage networks with public cloud storage.[3]

## Disaster Recovery

As the saying goes, "Disasters aren't planned," and that's why it's imperative to be prepared for anything from power outages to cyber-attacks, to natural disasters. It's also important to understand that different disasters require different responses, and everyone within your organization will need to understand their role and the actions they must take to minimize damage and restore operations quickly.

Creating a disaster recovery plan may seem like a daunting task, but it doesn't have to be. The first step is to assess the risks that your SMB faces. This includes identifying the types of disasters that are most likely to occur in your area and the potential impact that they could have on your operations. Once you have identified the risks, you can start to develop a plan to mitigate them.

A disaster recovery plan checklist should include the Recovery Time Objective (RTO) and Recovery Point Objective (RPO), hardware and

---

[3] https://www.ibm.com/topics/data-storage#:~:text=highly%20regulated%20data,public%20cloud%20storage

software inventory, personnel roles, a list of disaster recovery sites, remote storage of physical documents and storage media, disaster response procedures, identification of sensitive data, a communication plan for disaster events, physical facility needs, disaster recovery drills, etc.

It is essential to update the plan at least once per year and to run drills to test and improve its effectiveness. A comprehensive disaster recovery plan can help businesses minimize the impact of disasters and ensure the continuity of operations.

In conclusion, the top three areas of neglect are hardware, software, and backup and disaster recovery plans. Upgrading hardware, investing in cyber security stacks, and having robust backup and disaster recovery plans are critical to ensuring the continuity of business operations and protecting against cyber-attacks and other potential catastrophes.

It is also essential to take proactive steps to prevent IT negligence including ongoing cyber awareness training, policy and procedure plans for employees, and regular updates to disaster recovery plans.

IT negligence is a choice made by individuals and businesses that don't invest in the people and technological infrastructure needed to support, monitor, control, and protect technology. Neglecting your IT infrastructure can have devastating results. The good news is, you can begin taking care of your greatest business vulnerabilities starting today!

# About the Author

Brett Gallant has been active in the IT Industry for over 25 years and has been the owner of Adaptive Office Solutions, in Miramichi, Canada, since the spring of 2010.

Cyber Security is central to Brett's approach. He begins by running a comprehensive, multilayered technology assessment to identify gaps in security, in order to provide sound solutions that solidify the cyber security infrastructure for every client in his portfolio.

His clients include large construction and manufacturing firms to small and medium businesses. Brett's takes a customer centric approach, which means the customer is the focal point of all decisions related to delivering products, services, and experiences to create customer satisfaction, loyalty and advocacy. This strategic approach supports his client's goals of running healthy, growing and successful businesses through the use of secure, current and smooth-running technology.

Brett is active in the business and personal community; participating in cyber security groups and volunteering for his church, the Rotary Club of Chatham, and Camp Sheldrake, a summer camp that empowers youth through meaningful experiences, and develops skills in leadership and community service while increasing spiritual awareness.

He is also the founder of BPSA Scouting in Miramichi, which caters to the outdoor curious, adventurist, pioneer and explorer. Brett has five children, and he and his wife Alison have been happily married since the summer of 2009.

# The Importance of Securing Your Private Business Data

**By Linwood Wright**

Once upon a time, there was a successful Certified Public Accountant (CPA) named Richard. He had built a loyal clientele over the years and was known for his diligence, professionalism, and attention to detail. However, he never really considered the importance of securing his private and business data, believing that, as a small business, he was not a target for cyber-criminals.

One day, Richard received a seemingly harmless email from a potential client who claimed they needed help with their taxes. The email included an attachment that the sender said contained important financial documents. Without hesitation, Richard opened the attachment, expecting to see the client's financial records. Unbeknownst to him, the attachment contained malware that immediately infected his computer.

The malware allowed cyber-criminals to access Richard's computer and all the sensitive data stored on it. They gained access to his clients' personal information, including social security numbers, bank account details, and tax records. Richard was completely unaware that his system had been compromised, and the criminals went unnoticed for several weeks.

One morning, Richard and his partner began receiving frantic calls from multiple clients who informed them that they had been victims of identity theft and fraudulent tax return filings. They were shocked, and Richard quickly realized that their sensitive information had been stolen from his own records. He was devastated by the thought that he had unintentionally exposed his clients to such harm.

Within an hour of the first call, Richard faced another disastrous consequence of the data breach. The cyber-criminals had managed to infiltrate one of his business' bank accounts and withdrew significant amounts of money. This left Richard and his partner in a precarious financial situation, struggling to pay their employees on time. Their staff, who had always been loyal and dedicated, now faced financial hardships and uncertainty as they had to wait for their delayed paychecks. Some even contemplated leaving the company, searching for a more stable work environment. This further strained Richard's business as he not only had to deal with the fallout from the data breach, but also struggled to maintain employee morale and trust.

Richard enlisted the help of a cyber security expert to investigate the breach and secure his systems. The expert discovered the malware in his computer and identified the phishing email that had caused the breach. It is likely that the cyber-criminals targeted Richard's business specifically because it was an accounting firm and had access to valuable personal and financial information.

The data breach had severe consequences for Richard and his business. His reputation was damaged, and he lost the trust of many clients, some of whom chose to find another CPA. In addition to the theft of money, the breach resulted in additional financial losses as Richard and his partner had to invest in cyber security measures, hire a public relations firm to manage the crisis, and compensate clients who had been affected by the identity theft and fraud.

This unfortunate event served as a wake-up call for Richard. He realized that, as a CPA, he had a responsibility to protect not only his clients' sensitive data, but also his own. He took immediate action, implementing robust cyber security measures including data encryption, multi-factor authentication, and employee training on recognizing and avoiding phishing attacks.

Richard's story is a stark reminder of the importance of securing private and business data, especially for businesses who handle sensitive information. The consequences of a data breach can be devastating for both the business and its clients. Therefore, it is essential for businesses who deal with sensitive data to prioritize cyber security and safeguard their data from potential threats.

**How important is your business data?**

What is the one thing that, if it were gone tomorrow, would bring your business operations to a standstill and cause potentially irreversible damage? Asking business owners this question usually leads to one common answer – their data. Your data comprises all the information about your company, including its customers, finances, operations, trade secrets, intellectual property, personally identifiable information (PII), and so much more. Given that data is considered the most valuable asset of most businesses, imagine the catastrophic consequences if it were to fall into the wrong hands.

**Things have changed.**

In our technology-driven world, data security has become a top priority for both individuals and businesses. With the increasing amount of personal and confidential information being stored and transmitted electronically, the risk of data breaches and cyber-attacks has become a significant threat. As a result, there is a growing awareness of the need for robust data security measures to protect against unauthorized access, theft, or misuse of sensitive information.

While data security has always been important for businesses, it has become more critical than ever before. The rise in cyber-attacks, the collection and storage of large amounts of personal and confidential data, and the shift to remote work during the pandemic have created new and unprecedented cyber security challenges. As a result, businesses have had to adapt their security protocols to ensure that their employees can work from home while maintaining data security and preventing unauthorized access.

Remote access and VPNs have become essential tools for enabling secure remote work, along with employee training and education on cyber security threats. Cyber security audits and risk assessments have become crucial, helping businesses identify vulnerabilities and implement necessary security measures to protect against potential cyber-attacks and data breaches. Evaluating how data is collected, stored, accessed, transmitted, and secured is essential.

### Are you a target?

Many small and medium-sized businesses mistakenly believe that cyber-criminals exclusively target larger organizations. However, statistics reveal that, as larger organizations invest more in cyber security tools and strengthen their cyber security posture, hackers have redirected their attention towards smaller businesses which they perceive as more vulnerable to attacks. Alarmingly, research shows that 43% of data breaches specifically target small and medium-sized businesses, emphasizing the need for data protection across all organizations, regardless of size.

### The FBI is concerned.

There is no doubt that cyber-crime has become a major concern for national security, and the FBI has taken notice. The agency has recently identified cyber-crime as one of the biggest threats facing the United States, with the potential to cause significant economic and national security damage. They also expressed concern about a potential surge in cyber-crime targeting small businesses in America.

**So where do you start?**

To ensure data security, the first step is to identify and understand what critical data you handle, where it is stored within the organization, and who has access to it. This requires an assessment of all data collected, processed, and stored. By prioritizing the protection of sensitive data such as personal information, financial records, and intellectual property, appropriate controls can be implemented to secure these assets.

Based on my experience conducting Cyber Security Risk Assessments, I've found that every organization I've worked with was surprised to discover more sensitive data accessible on their network than they had initially anticipated. This realization can be alarming.

Once, a prospective client confidently claimed that her staff kept no sensitive information on their computers. However, after conducting a risk assessment, she was shocked to discover that there were 1,807 sensitive files across her organization, containing 7,610 social security numbers, 1,332 Electronic Fund Transfer (EFT) numbers, 34 credit cards, 2,933 driver's licenses, 768 email addresses, 896 usernames and passwords, and other confidential data being stored on their devices.

Many business owners assume that neither they nor their staff are storing sensitive data on their devices, or that cloud storage makes it inaccessible to hackers. However, after conducting an assessment, they often discover that personally identifiable information (PII) for their customers is scattered throughout their files. Additionally, they may find that their login credentials for various websites, including their banks, retirement accounts, payroll, and company business systems, are stored in their browser, making them easy targets for even novice hackers.

In reality, most business leaders are busy running their businesses and may not be aware of what files their employees handle, how they are transmitted, or where they are stored. Without the proper tools in place, they may not even realize if a bad actor is exfiltrating important company data, which poses a significant risk. Fortunately, there are tools available that can provide a real-time view of all activity on their files, including who has accessed them, when they were accessed, and what changes were made. Custom alerts can even notify them when specific files or folders are accessed, modified, sent or exfiltrated, giving busy business owners peace of mind knowing that they can easily monitor their files and ensure that their data is secure.

**Why is this important?**

A typical organization has a diverse range of employees with varying levels of access to sensitive data. The CEO typically has access to everything, including financial information, vendor contracts, and proprietary data. The CFO is responsible for all things financial, including payroll information, accounts payable and receivable, bank account numbers, company tax returns, and ACH and wire transfer information. Human resources handles sensitive personal information such as social security numbers, driver's license numbers, home addresses, phone numbers, email addresses, emergency contact, direct deposit, benefits, and medical information. Supply chain and product managers may handle confidential data related to product designs, manufacturing processes, vendor contracts, pricing information, inventory levels, shipping and receiving details, and other proprietary information. Salespeople may have access to business intelligence, sales processes, pricing, cost, margin, profitability, customer contact information, contracts, financial information, and credit applications. Other employees typically have access to login credentials for company email and business systems. It's important to note that these roles and access levels can vary greatly depending on the industry and the type of data being handled.

**What might happen if this data were to get into the wrong hands?**

If sensitive data gets into the wrong hands, it could lead to severe consequences such as identity theft, financial fraud, reputation damage, and legal liabilities.

Even the most benign information can be exploited by hackers who use seemingly harmless information, such as a person's name or job title, to trick individuals into giving out more sensitive information or clicking on malicious links. This is known as social engineering, and it is a common tactic used by cyber-criminals. For example, a hacker could use a salesperson's name and job title to impersonate them by creating a fake email and requesting sensitive information from a colleague.

In September 2022, it was publicly disclosed that Uber was hacked via a social engineering attack when an attacker tricked an employee into giving out login credentials. Despite a multi-factor authentication (MFA) policy being in place, the attacker compromised a Slack account and convinced the employee to approve MFA requests. This incident emphasizes the importance of training employees to recognize and respond to social engineering attacks, in addition to having security policies.

## What's the risk?

Failing to secure your private and business data poses numerous risks, including:

### Reputational Harm

The fallout from a data breach can have devastating effects. One of the most significant risks is the loss of credibility and damage to your brand's reputation. Once customers discover that their personal information has been compromised due to a company's failure to secure their data, trust is lost, and it's a challenge to regain. A loss of trust and negative publicity can result in reduced business and long-term damage to the company's reputation.

### Financial Losses

A data breach can result in significant financial losses for a business. The direct costs of a breach may include legal fees, fines, and expenses related to remediation efforts such as data recovery, equipment replacement, and notification of affected parties. Furthermore, there may be indirect costs such as a loss of revenue due to a decline in customer trust and loyalty. A company may also experience a decline in share value due to the negative impact on their reputation. In many cases, a data breach can cause long-term damage to a business's financial health.

### Regulatory or Legal Consequences

In an unprecedented move on February 1, 2023, the FTC fined GoodRx $1.5M for secretly sharing users' health data and prescription info with Facebook and Google, so users could be targeted with medication-specific ads, violating the FTC Act and Health Breach Notification Rule. According to Samuel Levine, Director of the FTC's Bureau of Consumer Protection, "The FTC is serving notice that it will use all of its legal authority to protect American consumers' sensitive data from misuse and illegal exploitation."

Consumers expect that organizations they do business with will responsibly safeguard their data – and they have regulations like this on their side. Many compliance laws now require organizations to do regular risk assessments. Companies who do not properly secure their business data expose themselves to potential legal action. Organizations are legally obligated to demonstrate that they have taken necessary measures to protect their customers' and employees' personal data in accordance with data protection regulations. In the event of a data breach resulting in the theft of personal information, individuals have the right to pursue legal action against the organization for compensation. Businesses may also face regulatory fines and sanctions for non-compliance with other data protection laws such as Health Insurance Portability and Accountability Act (HIPAA), the FTC Safeguards Rule, and the General Data Protection Regulation (GDPR).

### Loss of Data and Confidential Information

Losing access to data that is not properly backed up can be devastating if the lost data cannot be recreated. In some cases, businesses run the risk of unique intellectual property or confidential client information being irreplaceable.

Data that is breached often winds up for sale on the dark web. This can be disastrous for businesses, especially when it involves confidential information and Personally Identifiable Information (PII). Stolen customer data like names, addresses, and social security numbers can lead to identity theft and lasting financial consequences. Medical record breaches can lead to fraud, financial damage, physical harm, or emotional distress to patients. Loss of trade secrets or intellectual property can be a major blow to businesses that rely on these assets to stay competitive.

Compromised confidential information related to merger, acquisitions or other business deals can result in the collapse of those deals or significant financial losses.

## Operational Downtime

When a data breach occurs, it is important to treat the situation as the crime scene that it is. An investigation will need to take place to determine how the breach happened and the extent of the damage. This investigation is crucial if you hope to have your cyber insurance policy cover expenses such as ransom money, remediation costs, and repair expenses related to the breach. However, during this investigation, the company may need to shut down operations entirely, leading to lost revenue, lost customers, and decreased employee morale. This downtime can be especially damaging to small and medium-sized businesses that do not have significant savings or emergency funds. In fact, a high percentage of these companies go out of business within a few months of experiencing a cyber-attack. Even after operations resume, the company may continue to face disruptions while implementing new security measures to prevent future attacks.

**Ransom Payments**

Ransomware attacks are a growing concern for businesses that fail to secure their company data. This occurs when cyber-criminals hold your computers and data hostage and demand a ransom for release. The amount of the ransom is typically based on the perceived value of the information. If the ransom is not paid, the criminals may threaten to release information, causing significant harm to the business.

The consequences of a ransomware attack can be severe, both financially and for the company's reputation. If the business pays the ransom, it may be seen as supporting criminal activity, while refusing to pay can result in permanent loss of data. Moreover, these attacks are becoming more sophisticated, making it challenging for businesses to keep up with the latest security measures.

To combat this threat, it is essential for businesses to partner with a third-party cyber security firm. These experts can help businesses stay up to date with the latest tools and methodologies to prevent, detect, and respond to ransomware attacks. By taking proactive measures, businesses can minimize the risk of a ransomware attack and protect their valuable data from falling into the wrong hands.

### Stress

Experiencing a data loss can be a highly stressful event for both individuals and organizations. In the aftermath of an attack, there are many important tasks that need to be taken care of, including contacting customers, notifying vendor partners, informing employees, communicating with the media, and reaching out to your cyber insurance company. If operations are completely shut down, decisions need to be made regarding employee work schedules and compensation. Additionally, negotiating with the hacker or ransomware group, ensuring that data is properly backed up and recoverable, and seeking professional assistance are all crucial steps that must be taken. The enormous pressure and chaos surrounding a cyber-attack can make these tasks even more difficult and time-sensitive, and businesses who have undergone this ordeal would recommend other business owners try and avoid it at all costs.

**How can you prepare?**

Once you understand the value of your business data and importance of securing it, the next logical question is, how can you mitigate these risks?

Our clients choose to mitigate this risk through multiple layers of security including, but not limited to, Cyber Security Risk Assessments, a Security Operations Center (SOC), network security, authentication controls, password security, laptop security, encryption, firewalls, intrusion detection and response, vendor and affiliate management, and employee training. Proper disposal of data and devices that are no longer wanted or needed, authentication, data backup, and data encryption.

Perhaps the most critical component of securing your business data is ensuring that it can be restored quickly in the event of system failure, corruption, or loss. Performing regular backups can help businesses quickly recover from data loss and resume normal operations. By having backups of important data stored offsite, businesses may be able to restore data and systems, even if their primary systems are compromised or unavailable due to a cyber security incident. It is also important to regularly test backups to ensure that they are working properly.

Incident Response (IR) and Disaster Recovery (DR) planning are critical components of a comprehensive cyber security strategy because they enable businesses to respond to, and recover from, cyber security incidents and other disruptions quickly and effectively. Incident response is focused on responding to and containing immediate cyber security incidents while disaster recovery is focused on restoring operations after a major disruption.

## Conclusion

The ever-changing IT and cyber security landscape can make it challenging for organizations to keep up with the responsibilities of ensuring data security and system reliability. In today's business world, data security is more important than ever, especially with the increase in cyber-crime. My advice is to have tools, policies, and processes in place to monitor your technology environment. This way, you know where your data is stored, who has access to it, and when it is transferred or removed from your system. Many companies find that opting for full management of their IT infrastructure is the ideal decision, allowing them to benefit from comprehensive support and expertise in all aspects of IT management and cyber security. However, for organizations equipped with internal IT staff, partnering with a Co-Managed IT Services Provider that specializes in data security and offers 24/7 monitoring and support is an effective solution. By sharing the management burden with a team of experts, in-house IT teams can focus on more strategic initiatives while leaving the day-to-day tasks of keeping systems running smoothly and protecting against threats in the hands of third-party cyber security team whose focus is on security all day, every day.

# About the Author

Linwood Wright is the founder and President of My Tampa IT, a leading Cyber Security and IT consulting firm in Tampa, Florida.

My Tampa IT provides outsourced IT and Cyber security solutions for businesses, ensuring the protection of their sensitive data and the smooth operation of their IT systems.

With over 25 years' experience, Linwood has spent his career immersed in the world of technology. A pragmatic problem solver, he enjoys helping business leaders leverage technology to help grow revenue, reduce risk, and achieve a technical advantage over their competition. Having worked with hundreds of organizations throughout the course of his career, and being a business owner himself, he is uniquely positioned to quickly understand the dynamics of many different types of organizations and the challenges they face.

Linwood served in the Army National Guard prior to receiving his Master of Science in

Information Studies from Florida State University. A lifelong learner, he continued his education, earning several important technology certifications to become the trusted IT and Cyber security expert he is today.

When Linwood is not focusing on his business or sitting in front of a computer, he enjoys a very active lifestyle, traveling and spending time with his family.

If you would like to discuss the IT and Cyber Security needs of your business, Linwood is available to speak with you.

To contact or connect with Linwood:

Linwood.Wright@MyTampaIT.com

https://www.linkedin.com/in/linwoodwright/

# The Anatomy of a Cyber-Attack: A Guide for Executives

**By Chris Burns**

I grew up with sports, and to me, sports are the perfect metaphor for business. Yes, I know, you are probably thinking they are a cliché, or you don't love sports, but there's something about the competitiveness and structure of sports that just translates so well into cyber security. In this chapter, I break down two common attack vectors in totally made-up stories that are definitely not based on ANY real-life experiences (wink, wink). So, grab your favorite energy drink (mine's Monster Ultra), and let's jump into the playbook of the anatomy of cyber-attack!

## Business Email Compromise (BEC) – The First Half Attack

In the competitive arena of modern business, Championship Corp was a star player. Championship Corp's CFO, Mr. Lombardi, acted as the team's defensive coordinator, ensuring that the company's finances were always safeguarded. One day, Mr. Lombardi received an email that appeared to be from the team's star quarterback, CEO Ms. Summit. The email urgently requested the transfer of $257,000 to a new vendor to secure a game-changing deal. Without a second thought, Mr. Lombardi initiated the wire transfer, believing he had just scored a touchdown for the company. However, he had just fallen for a cunning play by a cyber adversary known as "Business Email Compromise" (BEC).

Now, we don't want our top executives to be outsmarted by cyber-criminals, do we? To help you understand and counter these digital trick plays, experts have developed a game plan called the "Kill Chain." We'll focus on the Unified Kill Chain but also make a quick huddle to discuss the Cyber Kill Chain and MITRE ATT&CK Framework.

## The Unified Kill Chain

The Unified Kill Chain is like the ultimate playbook that cyber-criminals use to score big against their targets. It consists of seven key plays (or stages) that can lead to a successful breach:

1. Reconnaissance
2. Weaponization

3. Delivery
4. Exploitation
5. Installation
6. Command and control
7. Execution

Now let's review the BEC incident and see how each stage of the Unified Kill Chain was part of the opposing team's game plan against Championship Corp.

**Reconnaissance**

Every good sports team scouts their competition, and cyber-criminals are no different. In our story, the attacker studied Championship Corp, learning about the company's roster, key players, and ongoing projects. They discovered that Ms. Summit and Mr. Lombardi were working on a major deal which created the perfect opportunity for a BEC attack.

**Weaponization**

With the target identified, the attacker crafted a deceptive email to trick Mr. Lombardi. This email was their secret weapon, containing a fraudulent request for a wire transfer. To make it seem genuine, the attacker imitated Ms. Summit's writing style and tone. Clever, right?

### Delivery

Now that the weapon was ready, it was time for kickoff. The attacker sent the email to Mr. Lombardi's corporate inbox, expertly bypassing the defensive line of spam filters and security measures.

### Exploitation

The success of the attack depended on Mr. Lombardi taking the bait. The attacker exploited Mr. Lombardi's trust in Ms. Summit and his desire to secure the deal quickly.

### Installation

In the case of a BEC attack, there's no malware to install on the target's system. But, if the attacker wanted to be extra sneaky, they could have included a malicious attachment or link in the email to plant malware on Mr. Lombardi's computer.

### Command and Control

If malware had been installed, the attacker would establish a connection with the compromised system to gain control and steal sensitive data. In this story, the attacker's primary goal was to fool Mr. Lombardi into initiating the wire transfer, so this play wasn't necessary this time.

### Execution

With Mr. Lombardi successfully tricked into sending the wire transfer, the attacker executed their endgame and vanished with the $257,000 meant for Championship Corp's new vendor. Touchdown, cyber-criminals!

## Ransomware – The Second Half Attack

In another high-stakes game of cyber defense, Last Place Inc. found itself facing off against an aggressive opponent: a ransomware attack. The company's IT manager, Mr. Patricia, was responsible for keeping the digital playing field secure. One seemingly ordinary day, he received an urgent email that appeared to be from a trusted software vendor. The email notified him of a critical security update that needed to be installed immediately. Eager to protect the company, Mr. Patricia downloaded and installed the "update" without a second thought. Little did he know, he had just unleashed a ransomware attack, and Last Place Inc.'s valuable data was about to be held hostage.

Now let's use the Unified Kill Chain to dissect this ransomware attack and learn how each stage played a role in catching Last Place Inc. off guard.

**Reconnaissance**

Just as before, the cyber-criminal began by scouting the competition. In this case, the attacker researched Last Place Inc. and identified Mr. Patricia as a key player responsible for maintaining the company's digital security. They also learned about Last Place Inc.'s software vendors to make their attack more convincing.

**Weaponization**

Armed with this information, the attacker crafted a deceptive email that appeared to be from a trusted software vendor. The email contained a malicious attachment disguised as a security update – the perfect weapon for a ransomware attack.

**Delivery**

With the weapon ready, the attacker sent the email to Mr. Patricia's corporate inbox, once again bypassing any defenses in place.

**Exploitation**

The attacker relied on Mr. Patricia's sense of urgency and responsibility to protect Last Place Inc.'s systems. By exploiting his desire to keep the company secure, they convinced him to download and install the fake security update.

**Installation**

As soon as Mr. Patricia executed the "update," the ransomware was installed on his computer. The attacker's malicious software quickly spread throughout Last Place Inc.'s network, encrypting valuable data and locking the company out of its systems.

**Command and Control**

With the ransomware installed, the attacker established a connection with Last Place Inc.'s compromised systems, allowing them to monitor the infection's progress and maintain control over the ransomware.

**Execution**

Once the attacker was satisfied that their ransomware had effectively crippled Last Place Inc.'s operations, they delivered the final blow: a ransom demand. Last Place Inc. was given an ultimatum to pay a significant sum in exchange for the decryption key that would unlock their data. The attacker had scored another touchdown in the world of cyber-crime.

## Lessons Learned

By analyzing the ransomware attack using the Unified Kill Chain, we can see how each stage played a part in the cyber-criminal's success. Understanding these stages can help executives like you make informed decisions about your organization's cyber security posture, allowing you to better anticipate and defend against future cyber threats.

In the high-stakes game of business, cyber security is a critical component of your team's success. By collaborating with your IT and security teams and using frameworks like the Unified Kill Chain, you can stay ahead of the game and protect your company from the ever-evolving threats of cyber-attacks. Remember, knowledge is power, and, in this game, staying informed is the key to victory.

## Comparing Kill Chains

Now, let's take a quick timeout to compare the Unified Kill Chain with two other game plans: the Cyber Kill Chain and the MITRE ATT&CK Framework.

### Cyber Kill Chain

The Cyber Kill Chain, developed by Lockheed Martin, is similar to the Unified Kill Chain but uses slightly different plays:

1. Reconnaissance
2. Weaponization
3. Delivery
4. Exploitation
5. Installation
6. Command and Control (C2)
7. Actions on Objectives

The main difference is in the final play, where the Cyber Kill Chain focuses on the attacker's actions on their objectives, such as data exfiltration or system sabotage. Both game plans are useful for understanding and defending against cyber-attacks.

## MITRE ATT&CK Framework

The MITRE ATT&CK Framework is like a comprehensive playbook of tactics, techniques, and procedures used by cyber adversaries. It's more of a reference guide than a linear game plan like the Unified or Cyber Kill Chains. The framework is regularly updated to include new threats and help organizations stay ahead of the game.

While the MITRE ATT&CK Framework provides in-depth information, it may be a bit overwhelming for non-technical executives who just want to get on with the game. The Unified Kill Chain and Cyber Kill Chain offer more accessible and streamlined approaches to understanding cyber-attacks.

### Free Agents Can Help

Understanding the cyber security game can be challenging and frustrating for business executives. That's where partnering with a Managed Security Services Provider (MSSP) could have been a game-changing move for both companies in avoiding these cyber-attacks. MSSPs bring to the table their extensive expertise, round-the-clock monitoring, and proactive defense strategies that can help organizations like Last Place Inc. stay ahead of the curve. With their in-depth knowledge of the latest cyber threats and vulnerabilities, MSSPs can identify and mitigate potential risks before they escalate into full-blown attacks. By providing continuous security monitoring, timely updates, and employee training, an MSSP could have helped to recognize and respond to the telltale signs of these cyber-attacks. Instead of going solo and risking defeat, partnering with an MSSP helps bolster your cyber security game plan and gives you a better chance of emerging victorious over cyber adversaries.

## Final Seconds

Now that I've analyzed the anatomy of a cyber-attack using the Unified Kill Chain, you, as a business executive, can better understand the tactics and strategies used by cyber-criminals. This knowledge will help you make informed decisions about your organization's cyber security defense and keep your company's assets safe from future attacks.

Remember: cyber security is a team sport. By collaborating with your IT and security teams, you can create a strong defense against cyber-attacks and ensure the continued success of your business. Just remember, it takes a great head coach to lead your team to victory (*cough* see my contact information below). And who knows? You might just become the MVP in your own corporate championship.

## References:

Kill Chain on Wikipedia:
https://en.wikipedia.org/wiki/Kill_chain

Unified Kill Chain: Raising Resilience Against Cyber Attacks: https://unifiedkillchain.com/

Cyber Kill Chain® | Lockheed Martin https://www.lockheedmartin.com/en-us/capabilities/cyber/cyber-kill-chain.html

# About the Author

In 2008, Chris Burns founded Techie Gurus to provide cyber security-focused IT solutions for small and medium businesses. In 2023, to better reflect the company's mission and commitment to its clients, Techie Gurus underwent a rebranding and emerged as "Your Cyber Team." The new name signifies the personalized and dedicated partnership they offer, ensuring that each client's unique IT and cyber security needs are met with the highest level of expertise and attention.

With over 20 years of experience and more than 50 IT certifications, including the coveted Certified Information System Security Professional (CISSP) certification, Chris is a respected authority and author in the cyber security field. He has worked with various enterprises, government agencies, and media outlets. He helps businesses understand and manage their cyber risks with a proactive strategy that protects their assets and reputation.

Contact Chris Burns at chris.burns@yourcyberteam.com or connect with him on LinkedIn at https://www.linkedin.com/in/chrismburns/.

Schedule a strategy session with Chris Burns and Your Cyber Team today and unlock the full potential of your company's technology and security needs by visiting https://YourCyberTeam.com

# Is Your Business Cyber-Attack Ready?

**By Bill Bunnell**

As technology advances and organizations grow increasingly reliant on digital systems, cyber threats have become a constant challenge for businesses of all sizes. Business owners, CEOs, CFOs, and executives must prioritize cyber security to safeguard their company's assets, information, and reputation. This chapter will explore the importance of cyber security readiness, legal requirements, incident response plans and how businesses can measure how ready their business is for a cyber security incident.

## Current Cyber Security Threat Landscape

The cyber threat landscape is continuously evolving, with new attack vectors and techniques emerging regularly. One of the most significant trends in recent years has been the rise of Ransomware as a Service (RaaS), where cyber-criminals provide ransomware tools and infrastructure to other criminals in exchange for a share of the profits. This model has democratized ransomware, allowing even less-skilled individuals to launch sophisticated attacks which has contributed to a surge in ransomware incidents.

Most cyber-attacks target employees as they are often considered the weakest link in an organization's security. Cyber-criminals use tactics such as phishing, spear-phishing, and social engineering to manipulate employees into revealing sensitive information, clicking on malicious links, or downloading malware-laden attachments. These attacks can lead to the compromise of an organization's network and data, resulting in significant financial losses, legal liabilities, and damage to a business's reputation.

In 2020 alone, the average cost of a data breach was $3.86 million. Furthermore, with the increasing interconnectedness of organizations and supply chains, a single breach could have widespread ramifications across multiple businesses. This highlights the importance of continuously adapting cyber security strategies and raising employee awareness to protect against evolving threats.

## Legal Requirements and Reputational Impact

Legal requirements for disclosing cyber security breaches vary across different jurisdictions and industries. In the United States, for instance, businesses must adhere to multiple regulations that require disclosure of cyber security incidents. One such regulation is the Health Insurance Portability and Accountability Act (HIPAA) which mandates that healthcare providers report data breaches involving protected health information. Another example is the General Data Protection Regulation (GDPR), a European Union law that also applies to US-based companies that handle the personal data of EU citizens, which requires organizations to notify supervisory authorities and affected individuals within seventy-two hours of becoming aware of a data breach.

Failing to comply with these legal requirements can result in severe financial penalties, legal action, and reputational damage. Moreover, the reputational impact of a cyber incident should not be underestimated. News of a data breach can erode customer trust, deter potential clients, and harm partnerships, leading to long-term financial consequences. In some cases, the reputational damage resulting from a cyber incident can be more costly than the immediate financial impact of the breach itself.

To mitigate the reputational impact of a cyber security incident, businesses should prioritize transparency and open communication with their stakeholders. This includes promptly notifying customers, partners, and regulators of the breach, outlining the steps taken to address the issue, and detailing plans for preventing similar incidents in the future. By demonstrating a commitment to cyber security and a proactive approach to incident response, organizations can help rebuild trust and mitigate the long-term consequences of a cyber incident.

### Measuring Cyber Security Readiness

Assessing an organization's cyber security readiness involves evaluating its preparedness to identify, prevent, and respond to cyber threats effectively. Business leaders can gauge their company's cyber security readiness by considering several factors including vulnerability to cyber threats, the efficacy of existing security controls, and staff awareness and training. Some key steps in measuring cyber security readiness include:

a. **Risk Assessments**: Performing regular risk assessments helps identify potential threats and vulnerabilities within the organization. This process involves evaluating the likelihood and potential impact of various cyber risks, allowing businesses to prioritize their security efforts accordingly.

b. **Security Controls Evaluation**: Reviewing and assessing the effectiveness of existing security measures such as firewalls, intrusion detection systems, and access controls, can help businesses identify areas for improvement and ensure their defenses remain robust against evolving threats.

c. **Penetration Testing**: Conducting penetration testing, also known as ethical hacking, involves simulating cyber-attacks on an organization's systems to identify vulnerabilities and weaknesses. This proactive approach helps businesses understand their security posture and take necessary steps to strengthen their defenses.

d. **Employee Training and Awareness**: As employees are often targeted in cyber-attacks, ensuring they have a thorough understanding of cyber security best practices and potential threats is crucial. Regular training sessions and awareness campaigns can help build a strong security culture within the organization and empower employees to act as a first line of defense against cyber threats.

By taking these steps, business leaders can gain a comprehensive understanding of their organization's cyber security readiness and make informed decisions about the allocation of resources and priorities to maintain a strong security posture.

### Cyber Security Insurance

Cyber security insurance is an essential component of a comprehensive cyber security strategy for businesses. It provides financial protection against the costs associated with cyber incidents such as data breaches, ransomware attacks, and other forms of cyber-crime. As the cyber threat landscape continues to evolve, having a cyber security insurance policy in place is becoming increasingly important.

Cyber security insurance policies can cover a range of expenses related to cyber incidents, including legal fees, public relations efforts, regulatory fines, and even the cost of ransom payments in certain cases. By providing financial support during the aftermath of a cyber incident, cyber security insurance can help businesses recover more quickly and minimize the overall impact on their operations.

In addition to the financial benefits, cyber security insurance can also encourage businesses to implement more robust security measures. Many insurance providers require policyholders to meet certain cyber security standards or implement specific security controls before granting coverage. This can help organizations establish a stronger security posture and reduce the likelihood of a successful cyber-attack.

However, it is important to note that cyber security insurance should not be considered a substitute for strong cyber security practices. Rather, it should be viewed as a complementary tool that provides an additional layer of protection for businesses in the event of a cyber incident. By investing in cyber security insurance, businesses can demonstrate their commitment to protecting their assets, employees, and customers while also safeguarding their financial stability in the face of ever-evolving cyber threats.

### Cyber Security Frameworks

Cyber security frameworks play a critical role in helping organizations develop, implement, and maintain robust cyber security programs. These frameworks provide guidelines, best practices, and standardized processes for identifying, assessing, and managing cyber risks effectively. There are several widely recognized cyber security frameworks, each with its own focus and approach. Some of the most prominent frameworks include:

a. **NIST Cyber Security Framework**: Developed by the National Institute of Standards and Technology (NIST), this framework is widely used by organizations in various industries. It focuses on five core functions: Identify, Protect, Detect, Respond, and Recover. The NIST framework is designed to be flexible, allowing organizations to tailor their cyber security programs according to their specific needs and risk profiles.

b. **ISO/IEC 27001**: This international standard for information security management systems (ISMS) provides a systematic approach to managing sensitive company information. Organizations that achieve ISO/IEC 27001 certification demonstrate their commitment to maintaining high standards of information security.

c. **CIS Critical Security Controls**: The Center for Internet Security (CIS) offers a set of 20 prioritized security controls designed to help organizations improve their cyber security posture. These controls focus on the most critical threats and vulnerabilities and are developed through collaboration among a diverse community of security experts.

d. **FAIR (Factor Analysis of Information Risk):** The FAIR framework is a quantitative risk analysis methodology that helps organizations understand, analyze, and quantify information risk in financial terms. It enables businesses to prioritize risks and allocate resources more effectively.

By adopting one or more of these cyber security frameworks, organizations can establish a strong foundation for their cyber security programs. Implementing a framework helps businesses ensure that they are following industry best practices and meeting relevant regulatory requirements while maintaining a proactive approach to managing cyber risks.

**CIS Security Framework**

The Center for Internet Security (CIS) offers a widely recognized cyber security framework known as the CIS Critical Security Controls. This framework provides a prioritized set of 20 security controls designed to help organizations improve their cyber security posture by addressing the most critical threats and vulnerabilities. Implementing the CIS Security Framework offers several benefits to businesses, including:

a. **Prioritization**: The framework emphasizes the most critical controls, enabling businesses to focus their resources and efforts on addressing the highest risks first. This approach allows organizations to achieve significant security improvements even with limited budgets and resources.

b. **Scalability**: The CIS framework is applicable to businesses of all sizes and industries, allowing for customization based on specific needs and risk profiles. This flexibility ensures that organizations can adopt the framework in a manner that best aligns with their unique requirements.

c. **Continuous Improvement**: The CIS framework promotes ongoing assessment and enhancement of security controls, helping businesses keep pace with the rapidly evolving threat landscape. By regularly reviewing and updating their security measures, organizations can maintain a strong security posture over time.

d. **Compliance**: Implementing the CIS framework helps businesses meet various regulatory requirements and industry standards, demonstrating their commitment to maintaining a secure environment. This can build trust with customers, partners, and regulators.

e. **Community-driven**: The CIS framework is developed and updated by a diverse community of security experts, including professionals from the public and private sectors. This collaborative approach ensures that the framework stays relevant and effective in addressing emerging threats and challenges.

By adopting the CIS Security Framework, businesses can establish a robust cyber security program that prioritizes the most pressing risks, adapts to changing threats, and demonstrates compliance with relevant regulations and standards.

## 3rd Party Security Assessments

Third-party security assessments play a vital role in ensuring that businesses have a robust cyber security posture. These assessments, conducted by external experts, evaluate an organization's security controls, policies, and procedures, identifying vulnerabilities and providing recommendations for improvement. By engaging an independent third party to assess their cyber security measures, businesses can obtain an unbiased perspective on the effectiveness of their security program.

One of the main benefits of third-party security assessments is the ability to uncover weaknesses that might not be apparent to internal teams. External assessors bring a fresh perspective and diverse expertise, allowing them to identify potential vulnerabilities that could be exploited by attackers. These assessments can also help businesses stay up to date with evolving threat landscapes and ensure that their security measures align with industry best practices and regulatory requirements.

In addition to identifying vulnerabilities, third-party security assessments can also help businesses prioritize their security investments. By understanding the most significant risks and areas for improvement, organizations can allocate resources more effectively, focusing on the initiatives that will have the greatest impact on their overall security posture.

Third-party security assessments can also demonstrate an organization's commitment to cyber security, which can be beneficial for building trust with customers, partners, and regulators. By proactively seeking external validation of their security measures, businesses can show that they take cyber security seriously and are dedicated to protecting their assets and stakeholders from potential threats.

Overall, third-party security assessments are an essential component of a comprehensive cyber security program, helping businesses identify and address vulnerabilities, prioritize investments, and demonstrate their commitment to security.

## Incident Response Plans and Tabletop Exercises

Having a well-defined incident response plan is crucial for organizations to effectively manage and recover from cyber security incidents. An incident response plan outlines the steps and processes to be followed when a cyber incident occurs, ensuring that the organization can quickly respond, minimize the impact, and return to normal operations. Incorporating tabletop exercises into an organization's cyber security program can help ensure that the incident response plan is both robust and effective.

Tabletop exercises are simulated cyber incidents that help organizations test and evaluate their incident response plans. These exercises enable teams to practice their response procedures in a controlled environment, identify potential gaps, and improve their overall preparedness. Conducting tabletop exercises offers numerous benefits including improved team coordination and more effective communication and collaboration during an actual cyber incident. This can help reduce response times and improve overall incident management.

Moreover, tabletop exercises allow organizations to assess the effectiveness of their incident response processes and identify areas for improvement, leading to more efficient and successful incident handling in the future. Participating in tabletop exercises helps employees develop the skills and knowledge needed to respond effectively to cyber incidents, improving their ability to detect and mitigate threats as well as enhancing their understanding of the organization's incident response procedures.

Tabletop exercises also contribute to raising awareness of potential cyber risks among employees and management, fostering a culture of cyber security within the organization. Lastly, conducting regular tabletop exercises can demonstrate an organization's commitment to maintaining a robust cyber security program, helping to meet regulatory requirements and industry standards.

By developing a comprehensive incident response plan and conducting regular tabletop exercises, organizations can enhance their cyber security preparedness, ensuring they are ready to manage and recover from cyber incidents effectively and efficiently.

## Outsourcing Cyber Security to Managed Services Providers (MSPs)

Outsourcing cyber security to a Managed Services Provider (MSP) can be a strategic decision for businesses looking to bolster their security posture while capitalizing on external expertise and resources. MSPs offer an array of cyber security services including threat monitoring, incident response, and security strategy development. Partnering with a third-party MSP for cyber security provides several advantages.

One of the key benefits is access to a diverse team of cyber security professionals who possess extensive experience and skillsets. By outsourcing to an MSP, organizations can leverage this expertise to ensure their cyber security measures align with industry best practices and the latest threat intelligence. In addition, outsourcing can be more cost-effective than developing and maintaining an internal cyber security team which can be expensive and resource-intensive. Businesses can access top-tier cyber security services at a more affordable cost, freeing up resources for other strategic priorities.

Scalability is another significant advantage as MSPs can efficiently scale their services to accommodate the evolving needs of their clients. This ensures that organizations remain safeguarded as they grow. MSPs often deliver round-the-clock monitoring services, providing continuous protection and prompt detection and response to any incidents. This 24/7 monitoring is essential for effective cyber security.

Moreover, MSPs are well-acquainted with industry regulations and standards, enabling them to assist businesses in maintaining compliance with applicable cyber security requirements. This support can help organizations avoid fines, legal repercussions, and reputational damage.

In summary, outsourcing cyber security to an MSP allows businesses to access specialized expertise, achieve cost efficiency, and maintain a robust security posture as they develop. This strategy enables organizations to concentrate on their core competencies while trusting that their cyber security needs are addressed by seasoned professionals.

## Conclusion

In conclusion, as the cyber security threat landscape continues to evolve, businesses must prioritize their cyber security readiness. Understanding the risks, legal requirements, and financial implications associated with cyber incidents is crucial for business leaders. By measuring cyber security readiness, investing in cyber security insurance, adopting suitable cyber security frameworks, and conducting third-party security assessments, organizations can build a robust security posture.

Furthermore, implementing a comprehensive incident response plan and conducting regular tabletop exercises ensures businesses are prepared to effectively manage and recover from cyber incidents. Outsourcing cyber security to a Managed Services Provider can offer organizations specialized expertise, cost efficiency, and continuous protection, allowing them to focus on their core competencies.

Taking a proactive approach to cyber security is essential for businesses of all sizes and industries. By investing in the right tools, strategies, and partnerships, organizations can mitigate the risks associated with cyber-attacks, protect their valuable assets, and maintain the trust of their customers, partners, and regulators.

# About the Author

Bill Bunnell is the Founder and CEO of Network Builders IT Inc., a Managed IT and cyber security Services company. Mr. Bunnell has over 20 years of experience in the IT industry. For the majority of those years, Bill has worked as a consultant providing network support for clients. Clients range from small to medium sized businesses to city governments, and publicly traded companies.

As CEO of Network Builders IT, Bill and his team have built an award-winning IT company which has been named as one of the top Managed Service Providers in 2023, 2022, 2020, 2019 and 2015. In 2019 Network Builders IT was named to the Inc. 5000 list as one of the fastest-growing companies in America. Also, Network Builders IT has won many industry awards from CRN and The Channel Company including the following awards, Pioneer 250, Tech Elite 250, and the Next Gen 250.

If you have questions about Cyber Security or Managed IT Services, Mr. Bunnell is available to speak with you. Go to https://nbit.com to set up a time to discuss your questions and needs.

# Real-Life Cyber Attacks

**By Dan DeFay**

On a Monday night in September of 2021, I received a desperate phone call from a friend of mine. I could tell immediately by the tone in his voice that something was terribly wrong. He told me that he was at his father's company, and they had suffered a ransomware attack that morning. After learning more details about the attack from one of the owners, I agreed to go on-site the following day to begin helping them recover.

This company that had fallen victim to a ransomware attack was a local engineering company with about 50 employees. Their annual revenue was over 6 million dollars, and they had three locations. Their customers were very large, publicly traded, companies and some well-known government organizations.

Upon arriving at their office, I could see the hopelessness on everyone's faces. I went to a few of the computers and could see their mapped drives to the server only had encrypted files that they were unable to open. Their accounting department was unable to access their

QuickBooks data. They could not log into their servers, including their Exchange email server that was currently sending emails with malicious links to their contacts.

They had outsourced their IT services to a local individual. He was unable to assist them because he had another larger customer that had also been hit with a cyber-attack. He was too busy assisting his larger client to help them. However, he was able to remotely disconnect the firewall tunnels to the branch offices, which was very helpful in containing the attack to only the main office. I also spotted a tape backup drive sitting on top of the server and a tape popped out labeled "Friday" which hopefully contained all of their data from the prior week, before the ransomware attack occurred.

One of the owners of the company contacted their insurance company, who was not able to help them as they only had business liability, no cyber liability insurance. My team contacted the FBI, and we began investigating the ransomware note provided by the attackers with the agent assigned to the case. The ransomware service used in the attack was LockBit 2.0, and the agent said there had been multiple reports of the same ransomware attack happening in the area at other companies since the prior week. After further discussion, the agent suspected the attack was from a group of cybercriminals operating out of Nigeria.

Later that morning, the owners of the company and my team met for a huddle to make some decisions on how we were going to respond to this incident. The company had no incident response plan and had never prepared for something of this magnitude. The FBI had offered to do the forensic investigation free of charge, but that would require confiscating all of the computers and servers for an unknown amount of time, without them being able to be used by the company. The only cyber defenses the company had were antivirus and firewalls. The company did not have any kind of remote logging or other methods of gathering information for the forensic investigation.

After reviewing all options, the decision was made to buy new equipment and replace the server and computers in the main office. Once the new server was setup, we would attempt to restore as much data as possible from the backup tape in the tape drive.

Under normal circumstances, ordering the new server and computers would have been a quick and easy process through Dell. However, since we were still dealing with supply chain issues during the COVID-19 pandemic, there was going to be at least 10 days of wait time for new computers to ship and 3 months for a new server!

I was able to find a very powerful workstation at a local computer store and use it as a temporary server. We were also able to purchase new NUC mini desktop computers and some laptops from Carbon Systems who worked with us to order and start shipping computer systems to us when possible.

We also decided to setup a new email service for all users with Microsoft 365 to restore control of their email and to shut down the servers they no longer had control over. While waiting for the new computers to arrive, we were able to get email services setup and running from Microsoft 365 for some of the critical employees to access their email from their cell phones.

A couple of the employees in the accounting department also told me that they kept weekly backups of QuickBooks on flash drives. We made sure to disconnect the flash drives, scan them for malicious files, and review the contents. One of them had a current QuickBooks backup for two of the critical company files. After setting up the server and restoring the QuickBooks data, the accounting department was the first department able to resume operations.

With the exception of about 20 files that were immediately quarantined for malware, we were able to restore all of their data from the backup tape to the new server. Luckily the attackers did not disable or delete the backup data before launching the ransomware attack.

In the end, the damage from the breach resulted in about 24 hours with no email and about 3 days with no access to QuickBooks and other files needed for operations. The company did not pay the ransom but spent over $50,000 in new hardware and incident response services from our firm.

Our company is now providing ongoing cyber security and IT services for the company. All of the servers and computers in operation prior to the attack were set aside for the FBI to retrieve. However, after six months, the FBI was still working through its backlog and had yet to start the forensic investigation. The company finally decided to forgo the FBI services and close out the investigation. Despite the downtime and expenses this company faced, this breach recovery was considered a success. Unfortunately, too many breaches don't end this well.

## Nation State Attacks

We are seeing an increase in nation state attacks. Unlike ransomware gangs, nation state attackers have other goals beside stealing data or impacting operations to hold a company hostage for a ransom payment. A few years prior to this incident, I interviewed the CEO of a local non-profit that shared her story with me. The FBI showed up at her office and immediately declared the area a crime scene. The FBI agents took control of the network and confiscated all of the computers. The organization was at a complete standstill and was not even able to go into their office for over a week. She later found out from the FBI that her computers had been controlled and used by a foreign government to launch cyber-attacks on the Pentagon. The Department of Defense blocks network traffic from specific foreign countries, and this attacker deliberately found weak networks with insufficient cyber defense protections inside of the United States so they could bypass the Department of Defense's network traffic defenses.

So many business owners think that their company is too small, or they have nothing that cybercriminals would want. The reality is that all businesses with computers and devices connected to the Internet, are always targets for cyber-attackers.

# About the Author

Dan DeFay is the Founder and CEO of SmartFirm IT, which services clients all over the United States. SmartFirm IT provides cyber security and technology management services for businesses, with a major focus on servicing law firms and other companies that handle very sensitive information.

Dan has over 30 years of professional experience. Prior to starting his company in 2015, he worked as a consultant for a legal technology company, worked as a network administrator in a large law firm, and served in the US Navy as a Fire Controlman, where he managed the NATO SeaSparrow surface to air missile system and all of its computer, electronics, and radar components.

Dan holds a bachelor's degree in Management Information Systems from California State University, Sacramento and several Microsoft and technology vendor certifications. Dan is a member of several cyber security and IT professional peer groups and frequently travels to conferences and seminars, staying current on industry news and trends.

Contact Dan and his team anytime for help with your cyber security or IT concerns at sales@smartfirmit.com.

# Cyber Security for Healthcare Providers

**By Ken Satkunam**

New York-Presbyterian Hospital and Columbia University – In 2010, New York-Presbyterian Hospital and Columbia University were fined $4.8 million by the Office for Civil Rights (OCR) for HIPAA violations related to the unauthorized access of electronically protected health information (ePHI) by researchers. The OCR found that the hospital and university had failed to implement appropriate safeguards to prevent unauthorized access to ePHI and had also failed to implement an adequate security management process.[4]

## What is HIPAA?

HIPAA (Health Insurance Portability and Accountability Act) security compliance refers to a set of rules and standards that healthcare providers and other covered entities must follow to protect the privacy and security of patient's electronic health information (ePHI). In simple

---

[4] https://www.hhs.gov/hipaa/for-professionals/compliance-enforcement/agreements/new-york-presbyterian-hospital/index.html

terms, it means that healthcare organizations must implement physical, technical, and administrative safeguards to ensure the confidentiality, integrity, and availability of ePHI. These safeguards include things like encrypting sensitive information, limiting access to patient data, regularly testing and monitoring systems for vulnerabilities, and having policies and procedures in place to respond to security incidents. The goal of HIPAA security compliance is to prevent unauthorized access, use, or disclosure of patients' private health information.

Staying HIPAA compliant is crucial for businesses that handle sensitive patient health information. To stay compliant, businesses must take a comprehensive approach that covers all aspects of their operations.

## How Do We Comply with HIPAA?

Staying HIPAA compliant is crucial for any organization that deals with protected health information (PHI). To maintain compliance with HIPAA regulations, organizations must implement certain policies and procedures that ensure the privacy, security, and confidentiality of PHI. These steps can help organizations avoid costly fines and legal repercussions resulting from non-compliance. In this regard, it is important to establish an effective compliance program that incorporates key elements such as regular risk assessments, employee training, and incident response planning. By taking a proactive approach to HIPAA compliance, organizations can protect their patients' privacy, safeguard their reputations, and ensure the long-term success of their business.

## Conducting a Risk Assessment

The first step in staying HIPAA compliant is conducting a risk assessment. A risk assessment is an analysis of potential vulnerabilities and threats to patient health information. The assessment should evaluate all aspects of the business, including administrative, physical, and technical safeguards. The most common tasks performed during a risk assessment include identifying all information assets, reviewing potential threats to those assets, evaluating vulnerabilities that could be exposed, and then prioritizing the risk of those vulnerabilities being exploited. The end goal of the assessment is to understand what important steps should be taken to reduce organizational risk.

My company performs dozens of cyber-security risk assessments annually across the United

States. These involve going onsite to observe behavior and review how data is handled while simultaneously running technical scans to uncover risky systems.

This important step sets the stage for all other activities under HIPAA, but it requires active participation in preparation, duration, and post-remediation. To get the best results, organizations should prepare all of their documentation ahead of time, identify critical assets, and involve important stakeholders early.

## Implementing Administrative, Physical, and Technical Safeguards

HIPAA requires businesses to implement a variety of administrative, physical, and technical safeguards to protect patient health information.

Administrative safeguards include policies and procedures for managing and protecting sensitive data such as access controls and incident response plans. This includes providing cyber-security awareness training for staff to help recognize risk and learn how to avoid it. A large and often tedious part of successful administrative controls is the creation and constant review of written policies. These should include acceptable technology use, disaster recovery, data encryption, password management, and how permissions are granted to information.

Physical safeguards include measures to protect against unauthorized access or damage to computer systems and data such as locking up laptops and servers. This also includes securing access to where sensitive data is stored and monitoring and managing staff access to that. Other areas include environmental controls such as fire suppression, and temperature and humidity control.

Technical safeguards include encryption and other security controls to protect electronically protected health information (ePHI). These are often the implementation of policies and include the real work of encrypting data, implementing software and hardware to protect information like firewalls, malware protection, and controlling who has access to data. Patching systems to fix vulnerabilities and logging and monitoring key systems are also important technical safeguards all organizations should have in place.

## Training Employees

Another important step for businesses is to train employees on HIPAA regulations and best practices for protecting patient health information. This includes educating employees on how to properly handle sensitive data and information, as well as how to identify and report potential violations. Training should be provided to all employees, including new hires and contractors, and should be done regularly to ensure that employees are up to date with the latest regulations and best practices.

Security awareness training for HIPAA compliance is more involved than standard awareness training for organizations not subject to HIPAA. On top of general best practices for recognizing and avoiding risk, HIPAA training involves the specific process of handling protected health information (PII).

There are many options to provide training including a software-based online course, webinars and seminars, in-person training, and tabletop simulation discussions. Our company provides several options for staff to get educated.

## Entering into Business Associate Agreements (BAA)

HIPAA requires businesses to enter into business associate agreements with any third-party vendors or partners that handle ePHI on their behalf. These agreements must include specific provisions to ensure that the vendor or partner is also compliant with HIPAA regulations. The agreements should cover items such as the handling and protection of ePHI, incident response procedures, and regular reporting of compliance status.

Some important things to include in the BAA are provisions describing how information can be used and disclosed, the obligations of the business associate, the safeguards the business associate will put in place to protect the information, and how any breaches should be reported and notified.

## Implementing Incident Response Plan

In the event of a data breach or security incident, having an incident response plan in place can minimize damage and help the business comply with HIPAA regulations. The incident response plan should include an outline of the procedures for identifying and reporting incidents, define procedures for assessing the severity of discovered incidents, and specific steps to be taken to contain and mitigate the threat. An often-overlooked step is to ensure that evidence is collected and preserved for forensics teams. In our practice, this is one of the most common mistakes technical staff makes. Finally, it's important to document the recovery and restoration process needed to bring critical systems and assets back online.

## Complying with the Regulations of the HITECH Act

The HITECH Act (Health Information Technology for Economic and Clinical Health Act) is a federal law that incentivizes the use of health information technology. HITECH regulations provide additional requirements for businesses that handle ePHI, such as the requirement to provide breach notification to affected individuals and the government.

Many of the safeguards we have discussed for HIPAA compliance apply to HITECH. However, there are a few differences. HITECH is an amendment to HIPAA that expands the law's privacy and security requirements while providing some funding for the adoption of "meaningful" use of electronic health record systems (EHR). In addition, HITECH introduced new breach notification requirements including mandatory reporting to affected individuals, Health and Human Services (HHS), and, in some cases, the media. If you've ever seen a story about a healthcare system reporting a breach, you can thank (or blame) HITECH for that!

## Conducting Regular and Repeatable Audits

Coming full circle, organizations should conduct regular internal audits. The initial cyber-security risk assessment only creates the baseline for all future audits. The threat landscape is constantly changing and everything should be reviewed quarterly but every year at a minimum. The audit should include reviewing policies and procedures, testing security controls, and reviewing incident logs. It is also a good practice to conduct periodic external audits by a third-party auditor to ensure that the business is complying with all HIPAA regulations.

## Why This Should Be Important to You

Being HIPAA compliant is of utmost importance in the healthcare industry where protected health information (PHI) is exchanged and stored regularly. The consequences of non-compliance with HIPAA can be severe, including financial penalties, loss of reputation, and even criminal charges in some cases. Maintaining HIPAA compliance is not only a legal requirement, but also a fundamental aspect of providing quality healthcare services while protecting patients' privacy and maintaining their trust. Therefore, healthcare providers and other covered entities must ensure that their practices and procedures comply with HIPAA's privacy and security requirements to protect patients' PHI and avoid legal and reputational risks.

**Memorial Healthcare System** – In 2016, Memorial Healthcare System, a hospital system in Florida, was fined $5.5 million by the OCR for HIPAA violations related to the unauthorized access and disclosure of ePHI. The OCR found that the hospital system had failed to implement appropriate safeguards to prevent unauthorized access to ePHI and had also failed to implement an adequate security management process. Additionally, it was found that a former employee had accessed and disclosed the ePHI of 115 individuals without authorization.[5]

## Compliance with Regulations

First and foremost, HIPAA compliance is a legal requirement for businesses that handle sensitive patient health information, and it demonstrates to customers, clients, and

[5] https://www.hhs.gov/hipaa/for-professionals/compliance-enforcement/agreements/memorial/index.html

partners that the business takes data privacy and security seriously. In other words, this is not optional!

**Protection of Sensitive Patient Information**

HIPAA compliance helps protect sensitive patient data and information, which is important not only for the patients, but also for the business. It is just the right thing to do!

**Legal and Financial Consequences**

One of the most important things to stress is that non-compliance with HIPAA regulations can result in significant fines and penalties as well as legal liability. The Office for Civil Rights (OCR) can impose penalties for violations of HIPAA regulations such as failure to implement appropriate security measures or failure to report a data breach. Not all penalties from the OCR are financial. Many times, organizations will be required to implement corrective action plans or take other measures to address the violation.

**Best Practice**

Being HIPAA compliant is not only a legal requirement, but it is also a best practice that helps protect against data breaches and cyber-attacks. It also helps businesses to comply with other regulations and industry standards. We often put organizations in two buckets; one is just trying to check the compliance boxes to avoid penalties, and the other is an organization that truly wants to be more secure. Be in that second group!

### Reputation Damage

A data breach or HIPAA violation can have a significant impact on a business' reputation, causing a loss of customer trust and business. This can be especially damaging for healthcare providers as the violation of patient trust can be detrimental to the business. Negative publicity can cause a public outcry, possibly attracting even more attention from regulatory bodies. Disclosure of patients' sensitive, personal, and medical information can be highly damaging to the affected individuals, leading to lawsuits and resulting in even more financial loss. In addition, people may lose confidence in the organization's ability to protect their information and may go elsewhere for services.

### Business Continuity

HIPAA compliance can also help businesses maintain continuity in the event of a data breach or cyber-attack. Having a plan in place to deal with such incidents can minimize the damage and help the business recover more quickly.

**Why don't organizations take this seriously?**

Despite the significant risks and consequences associated with non-compliance, some organizations in the healthcare industry may not take HIPAA compliance seriously. This may be due to a lack of awareness of the potential consequences of non-compliance or a belief that the cost of compliance outweighs the benefits. Some organizations may also lack the resources or expertise to implement and maintain HIPAA compliance practices, or they may have an outdated or ineffective compliance program. Additionally, some organizations may prioritize profits and operational efficiency over compliance, leading them to cut corners or overlook compliance requirements. Whatever the reason, failing to take HIPAA compliance seriously can lead to significant financial, legal, and reputational risks that can be devastating for businesses and their patients. Therefore, organizations need to understand the importance of HIPAA compliance and take proactive steps to implement and maintain effective compliance practices.

**Anthem Inc.** – In 2015, Anthem Inc., one of the largest health insurance companies in the United States, suffered a massive data breach that exposed the personal information of over 80 million individuals. The breach was caused by a cyber-attack that exploited a vulnerability in the company's IT systems and resulted in the theft of sensitive information such as Social Security numbers, birth dates, and addresses. The company was subsequently fined $16 million by the Office for Civil Rights for failure to implement adequate security measures.[6]

### Lack of Awareness

Some businesses may not be fully aware of their obligations under HIPAA or may not understand the potential consequences of non-compliance. They may not understand the importance of protecting sensitive patient health information or may not be aware of the specific requirements of HIPAA regulations.

### Lack of Resources

Some businesses may not have the resources, such as budget and personnel, to implement and maintain the necessary security measures and procedures to comply with HIPAA

---

[6] https://www.hhs.gov/guidance/document/anthem-pays-ocr-16-million-record-hipaa-settlement-following-largest-us-health-data-breach

regulations. Besides the time investment for producing policies, implementing safeguards, and training staff, healthcare organizations should assign a HIPAA Compliance Officer to coordinate and manage all of these resources.

### Cost

According to a survey by the Healthcare Information and Management Systems (HIMSS), the average cost of HIPAA compliance ranges from $100,000 to $500,000. This estimate only includes the direct cost of compliance such as staff time, training, and technology safeguards and does not include indirect costs like lost revenue or reputational damage. Some businesses may not see the value in investing in security measures and procedures if they don't see the direct financial benefit. However, the cost of non-compliance can be even higher than the investment in protection!

### Compliance as a Burden

Some businesses may see HIPAA compliance as an added burden on their already busy operations and may not see it as necessary.

### Assumption of Low Risk

Some businesses may assume that they are not at risk of a data breach or violation and therefore do not see the need for compliance.

### Lack of Regular Compliance Audits

Some businesses may not conduct regular compliance audits to ensure that the implemented security measures are still effective and to identify any potential vulnerabilities.

## Conclusion

HIPAA compliance is essential for businesses that handle sensitive patient health information. To maintain compliance, businesses should conduct regular risk assessments, implement administrative, physical, and technical safeguards, train employees, enter into business associate agreements, regularly review and update policies and procedures, implement an incident response plan, comply with HITECH regulations, and conduct regular audits. Non-compliance with HIPAA regulations can result in significant fines and penalties, legal liability, and reputation damage. HIPAA compliance not only protects sensitive patient health information but also demonstrates to customers, clients, and partners that the business takes data privacy and security seriously.

# About the Author

Ken Satkunam is a seasoned IT professional and the President and founder of NorthStar Technology Group, a leading information technology, and cyber security firm. With an impressive career spanning nearly three decades, Ken has held various roles, from technical support to the position of Chief Information Officer, for organizations with as many as 23,000 employees.

As the leader of NorthStar, Ken is responsible for providing visionary leadership and strategic direction to his team of passionate engineers. His guidance has enabled NorthStar to establish itself as a leading player in the IT industry, winning numerous awards while offering cutting-edge technology solutions customized to suit the unique needs of businesses.

Ken is also an acclaimed industry presenter and has contributed information security content to leading journals such as eWeek and DM News and compliance-regulated industry conferences across the United States. His expertise and insights have been widely recognized and sought after in the IT community.

Visit our website at www.northstartechnologygroup.com and to set up a strategy session to assess your company's cyber security risk, book at https://calendly.com/ken-satkunam/15min

**Contact Ken Satkunam at:**


Website: http://northstartechnologygroup.com

Email: ken.satkunam@northstar-tg.com

Phone: 701-237-9096

LinkedIn: kensatkunam


Book a Strategy Session: https://calendly.com/ken-satkunam/15min

# How Vulnerable is Your Business to Hackers?

**By James Forbis**

One of the hardest things for business leadership to understand is how vulnerable their companies are to hackers. Often this incredible risk to their business goes overlooked because it is difficult to grasp the scale of the problem. The FBI Internet Crime Report from 2022 showed that 800,944 cyber-crime complaints were reported to the FBI in 2022. This resulted in a loss of $10.3 billion.[7]

The scope of the problem can be daunting, and the methods hackers use keep changing. How can a business assess their vulnerabilities and prepare to deal with this growing problem? Using a program such as the NIST Cyber Security Framework can help, but it is difficult to decide where to get started. Here are five things to help you identify your vulnerability to hackers and ways to improve.

---

[7] https://www.ic3.gov/Media/PDF/AnnualReport/2022_IC3Report.pdf

## Gather Information

What you don't know will hurt you.

You cannot determine your cyber risk without gathering information about your business. There is a reason why it is the first step to the NIST Cyber Security Framework. You cannot protect, detect, respond, or recover from an attack on your business if you do not know what you are defending. This is not only the basis for determining how vulnerable you are to attack, but also the foundation upon which you will build your cyber defense. This is much more than an inventory of equipment. A successful audit should cover what data you have, how is it transmitted, how your team uses computers in all aspects of the business, and how much downtime the company can stomach. However, there can be a strong desire to skip this step. After conducting hundreds of audits, I've found that, in general, most companies are more exposed to hackers than you may have thought.

So where do I begin? At the very least should be a physical inventory of the systems on your network. This is both the hardware and the software. You should be looking for the following.

- What are the specifications and age of the system?
- What software is installed?
- Is the system/software up to date?
- Is it still needed?
- What data is stored on this system?
- How is that data accessed? Cloud or via network?
- Is the system publicly accessible?
- Is multi-factor authentication required?
- How critical is this system to the operations of your business?

The goal is not only to know what you have on the network, but also how it functions within your organization. Do you have a single computer that can bring your organization to a stop if it is not functioning? From there you can build contingency plans to get that computer running quickly in the case of an incident, or even better, create backups for that information so that the business doesn't come to a screeching halt in the event of a crisis.

An often-overlooked area of the business is the data the organization holds. What kind of information do you keep, does it have a value to hackers, and what would happen to your business if it got leaked? Everyone knows CPA firms, accountants, doctors, and lawyers hold a lot of sensitive information, but the data on your employees can be just as valuable. Payroll and employee information are gold mines to hackers as well as business bank account data. Criminals are looking to get paid; this data can be sold on the dark web, used to gain access to bank accounts, or to extort the business to not have the data released.

What should I be looking for when it comes to data?

- Where is the data stored?
  - Local PC, Network Share, Cloud Application
- Do my employees download data to their computers when they run reports?
  - The downloads folder of HR and Finance computers normally have a lot of data
- Who has access to the data?
- How is data transferred through the network? Or over the internet?
- Do you keep unnecessary data?

  - Old employee data, customer data, financial documents
- What data is necessary to conduct business?
- How long can you run without access to that data?

This is an extensive list, but it only scratches the surface of how data is used in business. Computer systems control the access to data, and data is what makes a modern business run.

Finally, we move to processes. What are the processes that are crucial to your business, and how can a hacker disrupt them? If your business relies on a CNC cutting machine, can a hacker take that system offline? How does money flow through your business? Can a hacker cause the flow of money to be interrupted or diverted into their bank account? What is the process to log into your business bank account and transfer money? Who has the authority to conduct wire transfers or change payroll information? What verifications are in place to ensure the information is correct and unable to be changed by unauthorized people?

The secret to information gathering is that it is never completed. As technology evolves, your business changes. Without having an understanding of how technology plays its role in your business, you will never be able to manage the risk from hackers. What you do not know will hurt you. That unpatched system that Bob in janitorial uses to order supplies can be the ingress point to a hacker shutting down your business.

## Vulnerability Management

I've identified vulnerabilities on my network; now what?

Hopefully, you have a better understanding of how technology fits into your business and now can make some decisions. One of the largest threats to an organization's security is simply the patch or update status of the computers and software. Hackers use software/hardware vulnerabilities to exploit your business. Their goal is to get money. They will use unpatched systems to gain a foothold on your network in the hopes of disrupting your operations or extorting money from you to keep your data from being leaked.

Now for the bad news. If you found end of life or end of support software or hardware in your information gathering stage, you need to remove those systems immediately. End of life systems are a favorite place for hackers to hide.

You need to identify what these systems are used for, find an upgrade path to supported software, or find an alternative process to cover this business need. Continuing to run software that cannot be updated is a critical vulnerability, and it means that it is only a matter of time until you are hacked. Establishing an upgrade plan should be top priority to any business as well as examining how the situation occurred so you do not end up there again.

The first line of defense against vulnerabilities is an automatic patch management system. This is a software package that will automatically update computer operating systems, server operating systems, device firmware, and some third-party applications such as Google Chrome and Adobe. These automated systems will update software on a schedule that limits the impact to the operations of the organization. The patch management goes beyond the built-in update software for Windows in that they allow for central management and checks and balances to make sure the updates actually work. They can also allow for the rollback of problem updates if they cause issues to the organization. Pair this with a vulnerability management software to scan the network for any missing updates, and you can tackle a large portion of the patching process.

Sometimes updates need to be installed manually. This can cause organizational downtime, so often the upgrades need to happen after hours. Priorities needs to be established on when the updates take place and how often these systems are updated. If everything is important, then nothing is. You need to have an effective strategy to deal with end of life, end of support, and vulnerable systems that cannot be updated on an automatic basis. Vulnerability management scanning can help identify these systems and place update priorities based on the severity of the vulnerability. These are normally rated on a scale from one to ten with ten being the most critical. Those critical updates need to be applied as soon as possible, even with the risk of creating organizational downtime. Organizational risk decisions can be made from there based on the severity of vulnerability, if it is public facing (IE can be accessed from the internet), the sensitive data on the system, and how its failure may affect the business.

Vulnerability management is a critical part of maintaining a healthy company and limiting your risk to hackers. Without effective vulnerability management procedures, it is not a matter of if you get hacked, but when and how bad will it be.

## Training

All this scanning and management is well and good, but how do the hackers gain access to your network?

The answer to that is most likely an end user gives them access. Phishing emails, hacked websites, business email compromises, Google results for fake support, phone scams, the list is never ending. More and more companies are locking down their networks, so the hackers attack what is easy – the end user. The fact of the matter is, your employees can be your greatest risk or, with an effective training program, you can turn them into your greatest resource.

If you are not training your employees on cyber-security then they will allow hackers access to your network. Our tests from running phishing testing on companies with no existing training program show that about 20% of the users click on the links or attachments. These tests are normally generic emails about something like UPS failed deliveries or Facebook account lockouts. Targeted emails specific to the end user, called spear phishing, normally result in ever better click through rates. After training users, click through rates should be below 5%. You will never get to zero due to human nature and needing employees to be able to access email and the internet to do their jobs. This is why you need a nested security platform as outlined below.

An effective cyber training program should be focused on education first. Some programs test employees on phishing and only train them after they click on a link. This makes the training punitive and does not train everyone. You do not know if the user didn't click on the link because they were great at spotting a bad email or because the testing message didn't apply to them. That user may not have their guard up for a real threat. A good mix of live trainings for all the staff normally produces the best results. Video training can provide general cyber hygiene, and live training can be tailored to the needs of the company.

Good training programs should empower employees to report things they see as suspicious on their computers and not punish them if they make mistakes. They will make mistakes, they are human. You want them to report to IT if anything suspicious happens, so you can respond to it quickly. An effective training program will lower your risk to hackers and make your employees excited to help fight back.

## Nested Security

I have a cyber-security training program, but my employee clicked something anyway. What now?

Cyber-security works best when it is a layered approach. In order to limit your risk to hackers, you need to make their jobs difficult. If they only have to defeat one security process, you are more vulnerable than if there are many layers. Let's take a look at the world of physical security as an example. Security started with a door and maybe a place to hide things. From there, locks were added, but criminals found a way around those. Then came alarm systems, managed alarm systems, security cameras, and now cameras that look at other cameras to alert if one is disabled. Not to mention safes and other concealment procedures. The idea is to make the criminal's job harder, so you are less of a target. The same is true for cyber-security.

A nested cyber-security approach consists of a combination of the following ideas.

- No users as local admins
- Strong password policy – 15+ characters
- Do not reuse passwords

- Acceptable use policies
- Email threat protection
- SPAM filtering
- Patch management with vulnerability scanning
- Employee training
- Endpoint Detection and Response (EDR) Antivirus
- Management for the EDR software
- Application Allow Listing
- Security Information and Event Management (SIEM) to detect, analyze, and respond to security threats
- Security Operations Center (SOC) team to manage and respond to threats as they happen

The list can get enormous, but the thought is to have policies, software, and systems in place to protect, detect, respond, and recover any threat to your systems. A business needs to continuously gather information to monitor if their approach is adequate at limiting their risk and evolving with the current threat landscape.

## Respond and Recover

One of the best ways to limit vulnerability to hackers is to be prepared. Hackers rely on chaos to get businesses to give them money. Being able to respond and recover from an attack will go a long way to keeping your business running.

Planning and policies are critical at this stage, as well as strong backups. You should use the 3-2-1 backup method to protect your company data. What this means is that you have three copies of the data, two copies of the data backed up, and one of those copies offsite. The industry has moved to immutable backups for the offsite copy. These types of backups cannot be deleted unless a period of time has lapsed. Having these "air-gapped" copies of the data, you also need to verify that the data you have backed up is accurate and functional. The worst time to test this is when you need the backup to save your business. A tested disaster recovery plan will help a business owner sleep at night knowing that they can recover in the event of a failure, whether it be accidental, intentional, or a threat actor.

Information gathering pays huge dividends here. By learning how your business uses its systems, you understand how data flows through the network and what is needed to keep your business running. Priorities can be set and redundancies can be planned to limit the impact of an attack. The best-case scenario is recovering a single end user computer, but you want to be prepared for a full network outage. Many of these nested security ideas are to help find out exactly what was affected by the hacker and how to recover from that situation.

Some policy documents that are helpful here.

- Business Continuity Plan
- Incident Response Plan
- Media Communications
- Disaster Recovery Plan

There is no single magic item that can limit your vulnerability to hackers. The truth of the matter is, being prepared is the best defense. Cyber-security is not a tool, it is a mindset. Knowing what you have, how it is used, and how to keep your business running is the best way to limit your exposure. From there, staying proactive on updates, keeping your employees informed, and having a plan to respond to threats will make the hackers' lives difficult. Working with a seasoned cyber-security professional can make this process much easier, allowing you to focus on your business.

# About the Author

James Forbis is a cyber security professional and business owner with over 30 years of experience in the IT industry. James is guided by a personal motto to never stop learning. That drive has pushed him to grow a company that is securing and supporting thousands of users. James is a Certified Ethical Hacker and he uses that knowledge to stay up to date with the emerging trends of cyber security and at the forefront of security for small and medium businesses in the Greater Cincinnati area.

Made in the USA
Monee, IL
04 November 2026

67384064R00108